THE PURSUIT OF HAPPINESS

A CLASSROOM CURRICULUM

TEACHER'S GUIDE

Robin Patterson

COPYRIGHT

A NOTE FROM GORDON LIVINGSTON

"*Robin Patterson's conversion of my book, TOO SOON OLD, TOO LATE SMART, into a high school course is at once flattering and very impressive. The principles contained herein - that we are defined by our behavior, that we are largely responsible for what we make of ourselves, that we need to be astute about whom to avoid and whom to cherish as we move through our lives - all are ideas of vital importance. I hope that those who partake of this curriculum, both teachers and students, will appreciate the work that has gone into creating it. We can never know enough about the pursuit of happiness.*"

-Gordon Livingston, M.D.

SECTION ONE

TO THE TEACHER

COURSE DESCRIPTION

PLAN IN ADVANCE - Guest Speakers

MOVIE SUGGESTIONS

HOMEWORK ASSIGNMENTS LOG

SECTION TWO

LESSONS 1-17
TOO SOON OLD, TOO LATE SMART CHAPTERS

1 If the map doesn't agree with the ground, the map is wrong.

2 We are what we do.

3 It is difficult to remove by logic an idea not placed there by logic in the first place.

4 The statute of limitations has expired on most of our childhood traumas.

5 Any relationship is under the control of the person who cares the least.

6 Feelings follow behavior.

HOMEWORK ASSIGNMENTS (5) + samples
- Three Questions
- Personality Traits
- Childhood Experiences
- Emotional Menu Project
- Journey Workbook/Pocket Folder Check #1

POP QUIZ #1 ON CHAPTERS 1-6

SECTION THREE

LESSONS 18-30

TOO SOON OLD, TOO LATE SMART CHAPTERS

HOMEWORK ASSIGNMENTS (2) + samples
- Personal Ad
- When I'm Old

GUEST SPEAKER OPTION

POP QUIZ #2 ON CHAPTERS 7-12

SECTION FOUR

LESSONS 31-45

TOO SOON OLD, TOO LATE SMART CHAPTERS

SECTION SEVEN

OVERVIEW

TO THE TEACHER

COURSE DESCRIPTION

PLAN IN ADVANCE - Guest Speakers

MOVIE SUGGESTIONS

HOMEWORK ASSIGNMENTS LOG

TO THE TEACHER

"Kindness - a willingness to give of oneself to another.
This most desirable of virtues governs all the others, including a
capacity for empathy and love. Like other forms of art, we may find
it hard to define, but when we are in its presence, we feel it."
Gordon Livingston, M.D., *TOO SOON OLD, TOO LATE SMART*

Practically everyone wants to be in a committed relationship, but why is it so hard to get it right? The divorce rate has been disheartening for a long time, and further complicating things is this high-tech, fast-paced age of cool devices that connect "friends" on facebook and on which we twitter away our time - now more than ever, there is a need for a course like The Pursuit of Happiness. When you think about it, no one really teaches us much about this most important aspect of our lives - how do we pick people and how do we be in a relationship, and especially, how do we be happy in our relationships? Our track record is sketchy. We make painful mistakes, often with serious, even disastrous, consequences; some of us learn from our mistakes, many of us don't.

This course is built on the premise that making good choices about the people we bring into our lives is central to the pursuit of happiness. It is designed to teach the skills and awareness that are requisite to making good decisions when picking friends and eventually a life partner. Because I agree with Gordon Livingston - whose book *TOO SOON OLD, TOO LATE SMART* is the course text - that this endeavor is too important to leave to random chance or trial and error, I took him up on his notion that we should devote some time to learning about how we pursue happiness within our relationships:

"To a large extent, this is an educational problem.
One would think that such an important area of human behavior
would be the subject of some consideration in the schools......
I could envision a curriculum constructed around the
general topic "the pursuit of happiness." p. 78

So, using *TOO SOON OLD, TOO LATE SMART* as the framework, I constructed this course. It is intended to be fun, challenging, interactive, introspective, and practical. While I am aware of other teaching techniques, The Pursuit of Happiness is intentionally discussion-based

TO THE TEACHER cont.

because the most effective way to increase our awareness of what we do and what's going on is to talk about it. Therefore, success is largely driven by your example and by your ability to get your students talking about what they do and what is going on in their lives. Be prepared to go first. The more closely your students look and the more your students apply what they're learning to their personal lives, the more likely that practical and real learning will take place.

At the end of the course, each student will have a Journey Workbook to keep and refer to, rather like a roadmap illustrating who they are, who they strive to be, what they learned in the course, what matters to them, and the quality of relationships they are inspired to create. The Workbook is intended to be a useful tool, a close-at-hand reference to help keep your students mindful, on a healthy course, and confident to make a course correction if necessary.

Readings, note-taking, writing assignments, creative projects, pop quizzes, role-playing, participation and attitude, guest speakers, a few movies, and a final exam comprise the curriculum and are the basis for grading. This Teacher's Guide is organized into sections - each section includes 6 chapters in Dr. Livingston's book, discussion points for each chapter, homework assignments with samples and other activities, and a pop quiz with answer key. There are suggestions for possible guest speakers and movies, a homework log to track assignments, Workbook checks to facilitate organization, as well as a sample pulling-it-all-together final exam.

Keep in mind that this is my interpretation and application of Dr. Livingston's book and how to teach about relationships and human personality. Use what works for you, what makes sense, what motivates you, and make changes when you need to. Make it real for you. Strive to get every student to laugh or smile, participate, and connect every single class.

Being happy and at ease in our relationships is a worthwhile pursuit. I wish you and your students a bold and fulfilling journey.

Robin Patterson

Robin Patterson

COURSE DESCRIPTION

COURSE TITLE: THE PURSUIT OF HAPPINESS

INSTRUCTOR: MS. ROBIN PATTERSON

COURSE DESCRIPTION: Learn about yourself. Learn about how you show up and interact with others. Learn to make more conscious decisions about who to get involved with. Learn to better recognize people to avoid and people to cherish. Learn to better recognize and cultivate important virtues such as kindness and empathy. Learn the critical thinking and conflict resolution skills that will increase your chance of having successful and happy relationships across your life.

LEARN HOW TO PURSUE HAPPINESS.

COURSE TEXT: *TOO SOON OLD, TOO LATE SMART* by Gordon Livingston, M.D., and the companion *The Pursuit of Happiness* Journey Workbook.

REQUIREMENTS: Pocket folder; an open and curious mind; an eagerness to participate in every class.

GRADE:

40% - class participation

30% - writing assignments, projects, quizzes, note-taking

20% - workbook and pocket folder

10 % - final exam

PLAN IN ADVANCE

GUEST SPEAKERS

Throughout the course, there are opportunities to invite a guest speaker to your class to discuss and share relevant experiences, and this requires some advance planning. The following suggestions are just that - suggestions. It is up to you how, when, and if you want to incorporate guest speakers in your curriculum. I personally believe it is a great way to illustrate the practical application of the ideas being discussed - bring in a real person who is living the experience. Be creative!

Around Lesson 29, during Chapter 12 ("The problems of the elderly are frequently serious but seldom interesting"), there is an opportunity to bring in an elderly person to talk about aging gracefully and with optimism. Find an inspiring example.

Around Lesson 35, during Chapter 14 ("True love is the apple of Eden"), you can consider inviting a person in the midst of a bitter divorce or a person who experienced a healthy divorce or a couple that is successfully married (25-30 years or more). Another possibility is to invite a divorce attorney to speak about his/her experience.

Just about any time in the course, you could invite a therapist or counselor to talk to your students about recognizing desirable and undesirable attributes, cultivating desirable traits, and healthy dating skills.

A psychiatrist could discuss personality disorders, perhaps in conjunction with viewing one of the movies.

MOVIE SUGGESTIONS

The movies listed below are just a few suggestions that could be worked into your class at your discretion. There is not enough time in the semester to watch all of them in their entirety, so you can either choose two, maybe three, to watch start to finish or just watch the parts that illustrate the point you want to make. In all cases, I strongly recommend that you preview the movie to make sure it is appropriate and acceptable. (Be sure to follow your school's policy for appropriate viewing and notifying parents, etc.) For example, "Who's Afraid of Virginia Woolf?" and "Fatal Attraction" are dark, disturbing movies, and some are rated R. A logical time to insert a movie, or part of a movie, would be after a pop quiz. Just be sure it works with the pacing of your class because watching a movie start to finish and allowing time for discussion that reinforces concepts being covered in class will likely require 3-4 class periods.

(The reviews below are from the Netflix website.)

AS GOOD AS IT GETS 1992, rated PG-13, 138 minutes. When acerbic, reclusive and obsessive-compulsive author Melvin Udall (Jack Nicholson) lets stressed-out single mom and waitress Carol Connelly (Helen Hunt) and gay neighbor Simon Bishop (Greg Kinnear) and his dog into his life, profound changes await them all in this touching dramedy. Nominated for 7 Academy Awards.

FATAL ATTRACTION 1987, rated R, 119 minutes. Happily married New York lawyer Dan Gallagher (Michael Douglas) finds himself attracted to his colleague Alex (Glenn Close), and the two enjoy a passionate tryst while Dan's wife and child are away. But the one-night stand comes back to haunt Dan when Alex refuses to let him go and begins to stalk him and his family. Just how far will she go to get what she wants?

HE'S JUST NOT THAT INTO YOU 2009, rated PG-13, 129 minutes. Follow this all-star cast of characters as they deal with the pitfalls of love and human interaction. Set in Baltimore, the film moves swiftly between several storylines and characters brought to life by Jennifer Aniston, Drew Barrymore, Scarlett Johansson, Ginnifer Goodwin, Ben Affleck, Jennifer Connelly and Justin Long.

JUST WRIGHT 2010, rated PG, 101 minutes. Good-hearted physical therapist Leslie Wright (Queen Latifah) is looking for romance but keeps finding duds until she meets professional basketball player Scott McKnight (Common). When Scott suffers a major injury, it's up to Leslie to save his career. Leslie and Scott become close as they work together, but Leslie's

MOVIE SUGGESTIONS cont.

beautiful, gold-digging childhood chum - who is also Scott's estranged girlfriend - threatens their relationship.

ORDINARY PEOPLE 1980, rated R, 124 minutes. Everything is in its proper place in the Jarrett household - except the past. Mary Tyler Moore plays a repressed mother whose favorite son has died, leaving her with another (Timothy Hutton) she can barely tolerate. Robert Redford directed the movie and it won four Academy Awards.

SHALLOW HAL 2001, rated PG-13, 113 minutes. Hal (Jack Black) is a terminal bachelor obsessed with scoring a knockout babe. A chance encounter in an elevator with a self-help guru imbues Hal with the (hallucinatory) power to see people's inner beauty over their outer shell. Soon he finds true love in Rosie, a 400-pound social worker who appears to Hal in the lithe form of Gwyneth Paltrow.

THE BUCKET LIST 2007, rated PG-13, 97 minutes. When corporate mogul Edward Cole (Jack Nicholson) and mechanic Carter Chambers (Morgan Freeman) wind up in the same hospital room, the two terminally ill men bust out of the cancer ward with a plan to experience life to the fullest before they kick the bucket. In a race against the reaper, the new friends hit the tables in Monte Carlo, down obscene amounts of caviar, and tear up the road in supercharged cars. It's a comic caper.

27 DRESSES 2007, rated PG-13, 105 minutes. Tired of being a perpetual bridesmaid after helping 27 friends tie the knot, altruistic Jane (Katherine Heigl) finds herself facing her worst nightmare as her younger sister (Malin Akerman) announces her engagement to the man Jane secretly adores. But when Jane meets the charming Kevin (James Marsden), will she beat her sibling to the altar? Edward Burns and Judy Greer also star in this breezy romantic comedy.

WHEN HARRY MET SALLY 1989, rated R, 96 minutes. Can men and women be friends without sex getting in the way? Womanizing, neurotic Harry (Billy Crystal) and ambitious, equally neurotic Sally (Meg Ryan) are friends who resist sexual attraction to maintain their friendship - a relationship always teetering on the brink of love. As the two draw closer, the question resurfaces: Can they stay just pals?

WHO'S AFRAID OF VIRGINIA WOOLF? 1966, unrated, 131 minutes. On a serene New England campus, an emasculated professor (Richard Burton) and his rancorous wife (Elizabeth

MOVIE SUGGESTIONS cont.

Taylor) turn an evening of cocktails into an unrelenting onslaught of wrenching disclosures and bellowed epithets. Soon the couple's guests - a junior professor (George Segal) and his colorless wife (Sandy Dennis) get sucked into the vortex of the warring duo's unbounded fury and endless antipathy.

NOTES:

....

....

....

....

....

....

....

....

....

....

....

....

....

....

....

....

....

....

HOMEWORK ASSIGNMENTS LOG

LESSON 1	Three Questions	50 points
LESSON 3	Personality Traits	50 points
LESSON 10	Childhood Experiences	50 points
LESSON 14	Emotional Menu Project	100 points
LESSON 14	Journey Workbook Check #1	50 points
LESSON 24	Personal Ad	50 points
LESSON 28	When I'm Old	50 points
LESSON 32	Optimist or Pessimist?	50 points
LESSON 34	Who To Pick Letter	50 points
LESSON 36	Happiness-producing vs. Bad News	100 points
LESSON 48	Cognitive Dissonance	50 points
LESSON 50	Journey Workbook Check #2	50 points
LESSON 53	Letter about Criticism or Gratitude	50 points
LESSON 59	100 Words on Meditation	50 points
LESSON 61	Role Models	50 points
LESSON 63	Eulogy	50 points
LESSON 66	Jokes	50 points
LESSON 69	Survival Strategies Poster	100 points
LESSON 72	Epitaph	50 points
LESSON 76	Journey Workbook Check #3	50 points
	Pop Quiz #1	50 points
	Pop Quiz #2	50 points
	Pop Quiz #3	50 points
	Pop Quiz #4	50 points
	Pop Quiz #5	50 points
	Final Exam	100 points
	TOTAL POINTS POSSIBLE	1,500 points

OVERVIEW

LESSONS 1-17

TOO SOON OLD, TOO LATE SMART CHAPTERS

1   If the map doesn't agree with the ground, the map is wrong.

2   We are what we do.

3   It is difficult to remove by logic an idea not placed there by logic in the first place.

4   The statute of limitations has expired on most of our childhood traumas.

5   Any relationship is under the control of the person who cares the least.

6   Feelings follow behavior.

HOMEWORK ASSIGNMENTS (5) + samples
- Three Questions
- Personality Traits
- Childhood Experiences
- Emotional Menu Project
- Journey Workbook/Pocket Folder Check #1

POP QUIZ #1 ON CHAPTERS 1-6

LESSON 1

INTRODUCE yourself, background, experience, education, etc...and why you want to teach this class, why it's important; share some things about yourself. Create a fun hook - YouTube clip or candid camera or America's Funniest Videos or a cartoon - something fun and relevant.

DISCUSS Why did you sign up for this? What piqued your curiosity?

COURSE OVERVIEW AND REQUIREMENTS: class participation; readings from text; writing assignments and projects; an organized and complete Journey Workbook and folder; note-taking; pop quizzes and final exam.

TOPICS: definition of love, personality disorders, recognizing desirable and undesirable personality traits, parenting styles, birth order, expanding communication skills, conflict resolution, and critical thinking skills to name a few... Really the course is about increasing your awareness of human behavior - who we are, what we do, and why we do it.

GO TO AND READ TO THE STUDENT in the Journey Workbook.

GO TO AND READ the HOMEWORK ASSIGNMENTS LOG.

GO TO the TITLE PAGE in the Journey Workbook. Optional/extra credit - add some artwork relevant to you and your pursuit of happiness.

PASS OUT course text - *TOO SOON OLD, TOO LATE SMART,* record book numbers - you lose it, you buy it; option to purchase at course conclusion.

BEGIN DISCUSSION OF HAPPINESS, LOVE, AND COMMUNICATION - how do you define it; how do you recognize it; how do you do it; examples in your life.
Who do you talk to? Describe the dialogue - the conversation *is* the relationship.

HOMEWORK

Go to Lesson 1 Homework in the Journey Workbook, explain directions.
Due tomorrow, 50 points.

LESSON 1 cont.

TO THE STUDENT

You might be asking yourself, "What on earth is this class - The Pursuit of Happiness - going to teach me?" It's an elective course, related to psychology, maybe an easy 'A'. But are you wondering if and how it will be relevant to your everyday life? I remember high school and that somewhat cynical question, "How is this going to help me in life?" Really, what's the point?

Perhaps somewhere along the way you've been told that it's important to "be happy" and that it's your relationships in life - more than your work, your stuff, or your hobbies - that really make the difference in how happy you are. But what does "being happy" in a relationship mean? What does it look like and how do we do it?

People come in and out of our lives, and one of the most important things we do during our lifetime is decide with whom we want to be in a relationship. What's amazing is that no one really teaches us how to do this - we think we know, perhaps just by observation and subconscious osmosis, and we rarely ask how it's done (how embarrassing!), so we're mostly left to our own devices to figure it out. Often it's not pretty, and let's be honest - this isn't something you can learn on facebook or twitter.

The point of this course is to teach you the skills and awareness to make good decisions when picking friends and eventually a life partner, thereby increasing your chances of having successful, happy relationships across your life. I believe it's too important to leave to random chance or trial and error. I believe being happy isn't as complicated or difficult as the divorce rate would have you think. I believe making good choices about the people we bring into our lives is central to the pursuit of happiness. Therefore, I believe we should devote some time to learning about how and why we make these decisions.

Because of a small but mighty book titled *TOO SOON OLD, TOO LATE SMART* by Gordon Livingston, I constructed the course you are about to take. The course is built around the ideas in his book. Topics include defining love, recognizing desirable and undesirable character traits, parenting styles, birth order, growing old, communication, and conflict resolution

LESSON 1 cont.

skills. I ask that you show up prepared, with an open, curious mind, a sense of humor, and a willingness to participate.

Yes, it's personal. We'll be talking about life in general and yours in particular, and as with so many worthwhile endeavors in life, the more you put into this course, the more you'll get out of it. My goal is to make it relevant, meaningful, and fun. Who knows, twenty or thirty years from now, you may just look back on this course as one that made a significant difference in the quality of your life.

To assist you on your journey of pursuing happiness, I created this Journey Workbook. It includes pages for note-taking and reflection, homework assignments, course handouts, and creative project assignments. In the pocket folder you provide, you will keep your quizzes, homework and creative assignments, and final exam. My objective is to provide an organizational tool that will make this information easily accessible if you choose to return to it to be reminded, to refresh, or restart. You'll be able to look back to your roadmap at any time and use the extra pages at the back to reflect and write an update on how it's going and what you're learning.

I would be happy to hear from you with your feedback and suggestions - feel free to contact me.

I wish you a bold and fulfilling journey!

Robin Patterson

Robin Patterson

LESSON 1 // HOMEWORK

THREE QUESTIONS
Due tomorrow, 50 points.

On a separate sheet of paper, answer the following three questions in complete sentences. Proper grammar and clear thinking always count. Handwritten is acceptable as long as it is legible.

1.   Describe your family and who currently lives with you at home. List siblings and ages, pets too, if you want. Write a brief snapshot of your family life.

2.   Read through the "Contents" of *TOO SOON OLD, TOO LATE SMART*. List the three chapters that piqued your curiosity and explain why.

3.   In one sentence, write a definition of love. Be prepared to share and explain what you mean.

NOTE ABOUT HOMEWORK
Completed/graded homework assignments will be kept in students' Pocket Folder. Not only does this step facilitate organization, it is required for the workbook and pocket folder checks that occur three times during the course. Doing homework on a separate sheet of paper, rather than in the workbook, makes it easier for you to collect and grade.

LESSON 1 // HOMEWORK cont.

THREE QUESTIONS HOMEWORK SAMPLE

1. I am a divorced mother of two sons, ages 16 and 13. We live in an old farmhouse with twenty acres, a big red barn, a creek, gardens, and animals, on the outskirts of town. Chugs, a black lab, and Buddy, a golden retriever, contribute to the calm or chaos, as the case may be. Bugs, the bunny, munches carrots and stuff in his hutch outside. A small flock of goofy chickens provides entertainment and excellent eggs. Then there's Chancho, the adorable miniature donkey, who is friendly as can be and loves to bust rodeo moves, and his two pygmy goat companions, Pebbles and BamBam. My sons primarily live with me and occasionally spend time with their dad. I'm also a first-born daughter, middle child. I have an older and younger brother. My parents divorced when I was 12 years old.

2. "True love is the apple of Eden" (ch 14) - how do we recognize/find true love? how do we know?

   "Parents have limited ability..." (ch 26) - I want to do a good job raising my boys and parenting is a huge responsibility.

   "There is nothing more pointless..." (ch 18) - how can I catch myself from being on autopilot, from doing the same thing over and over when I know it's stupid or wrong or doesn't work?

3. Love is the ease that comes when you feel safe in all your emotions. I can be and feel whatever I need to be and feel and it's okay. I'm not afraid. I know and trust myself and the person/people I'm with.

LESSON 2

EXPECTATIONS EVERYDAY: Journey Workbook, ready for note-taking, homework complete, course text.

COLLECT HOMEWORK to grade and return tomorrow. Ask first-borns to raise their hands... babies....only children...parents together/divorced/getting divorced....live with mom/dad/other... pets....

GET 'EM TALKING - start getting to know them! Discuss birth order; how it influences personality; what you learn going first, middle or last.

DISCUSS/DEFINE: LOVE. Look for ease, safety, and kindness. Ability to communicate - who do you talk to? The conversation is the relationship. Also trust, honesty, empathy, respect, compatible interests/values, attraction, etc. You get what you give - you can't expect what you don't offer. Create a class definition.

READ ALOUD TOGETHER CHAPTER 1, *TOO SOON OLD, TOO LATE SMART*

If the map doesn't agree with the ground, the map is wrong.

POINTS FOR DISCUSSION

1. How do we learn? How do we get the maps in our head to conform to reality? Ideally, we learn as we grow, mostly from our parents. Unfortunately, we aren't always receptive to these lessons and often our parents' lives suggest to us they have little of importance to convey. So much of our learning comes to us through painful trial and error. (p. 2)

2. Consider an important life task - choosing and keeping a mate. A high divorce rate shows that we're not very good at this task, and often our parents' relationship is not reassuring. Often those whose parents are still together describe them as living a boring or conflicted coexistence that makes economic sense but lacks anything resembling excitement or emotional satisfaction. (p. 2)

3. Serial monogamy is not a very good model for child rearing since it doesn't provide the stability and security that children need in order to begin to construct their maps of how the world works. (p. 3)

4. So how do we choose? We must learn about personality and desirable/undesirable attributes. (p. 3)

LESSON 2 cont.

5. Personality = habitual ways of thinking, feeling and relating to others. (p. 3)

6. Desirable and undesirable attributes are not randomly distributed; they exist as constellations of traits that are recognizable and reasonably stable over time. (p. 4)

7. People to avoid - personality disorders: histrionic, narcissistic, dependent, borderline. Define, explain. Learn to recognize!

8. Know the virtuous character traits you want to nurture in yourselves and seek in your friends and lovers. KINDNESS is at the top of the list, a willingness to give of oneself to another. (p. 4)

9. <u>GOAL</u>: to construct a reliable guide that allows us to avoid those who are not worthy of our time and trust, and to embrace those who are. (p. 5)

10. We must learn to recognize the signs that our always-tentative map is faulty (sadness, anger, betrayal, impatience, surprise, disorientation, silence, etc.) and be willing to make corrections in our mental instrument of navigation so we don't fall into unhealthy repetitive patterns. This opportunity to learn and get it right is the only consolation for the pain of trial and error learning. (p. 5)

NOTE

Points for discussion are the chapter highlights intended to become part of the students' notes. Allow sufficient time every class for them to write them down, or occasionally create handouts or power points. Remember, part of their grade is based on their note-taking. It's okay to help them!

LESSON 3

RETURN GRADED HOMEWORK. Keep in Pocket Folder.

EXPECTATIONS FOR NOTE-TAKING.

CONTINUE DISCUSSION from Lesson 2, points 1 - 10.

DISCUSS/DESCRIBE parenting styles - authoritative vs. permissive - and how the different styles influence the map you create in your head. What story or theme do you learn from different types of parenting? Controlling, cooperative, never have time, don't listen, don't care, patient, available, happy, depressed, angry, never good enough, etc. Play out a style.

HOMEWORK

Go to Lesson 3 Homework in the Journey Workbook, explain directions.

Due tomorrow, 50 points.

Use rest of class time to begin.

NOTES:

....

....

....

....

....

....

....

....

....

....

....

....

LESSON 3 // HOMEWORK

PERSONALITY TRAITS
Due tomorrow, 50 points.

Write down three - or more - personality traits that reflect some of your habitual patterns of thinking, feeling, and relating to others. Describe how you "do" the trait. Include both positive and negative patterns. Recognizing what you do is the first step to understanding if the pattern is serving you well, if it's a habit you want to keep or stop. If you want, ask your family or friends - sometimes we don't see ourselves accurately!!

Be prepared to share your homework in a class discussion tomorrow.

Pay more attention to kindness.

NOTES:

....

....

....

....

....

....

....

....

....

....

....

....

LESSON 3 // HOMEWORK cont.

PERSONALITY TRAITS HOMEWORK SAMPLE

1. Generally, I'm an enthusiastic person. In fact, "enthusiastic" was the adjective I chose to describe myself on a college application essay some 30 years ago. New ideas, mundane chores, whatever task is at hand, I find that I feel happier and things go more smoothly with a positive, upbeat attitude. Enthusiasm makes me feel light on my feet, more open and curious, more patient - and it's contagious! Whatever it is I have to spend my time on, it's much more enjoyable if I'm enthusiastic and put some positive energy into it....and when I'm enjoying myself, I do a better job, take more care, pay more attention. It's just more fun, a better way to live, and after all these years I can honestly say enthusiasm works!

2. As a mom and a teacher I have cultivated the trait of patience. Always taking care of others "right now" is tiring and not always fun or what I want to do, but it's what being a mom is all about, especially during those early years. If I stay patient and deal with one thing at a time, I can offer good help/support and thorough explanations for those seemingly endless questions, and be a clear role model for positive behavior. If I lose my patience - which of course I sometimes do - I'm not a good example, I'm not teaching my kids what I want them to learn. Impatience, anger, edgy voice, and tight body language are not what I want to show very often. Being patient allows me to take advantage of more of the teachable moments that life and children present. People who were significant role models of patience were my mom, my 6th grade teacher, and my high school basketball coach. Patience begets good things.

3. One personality trait I don't particularly like is my tendency to get quiet when I'm feeling disconnected from someone. I don't talk very much, my mood feels low or heavy, my voice isn't energized, I don't feel like smiling, and I need some space. A disconnect happens when someone says or does an unkind, insensitive thing, or when I misinterpret someone/something and it just hits me wrong. Sometimes there's a subconscious connection to the past. In any case, I practice speaking up, not letting the silence drag on - I gather my thoughts, I let go, I lighten up, I turn towards instead of away, I try to describe what I'm feeling so I'm not confusing. I'm not trying to

LESSON 3 // HOMEWORK cont.

completely stop going quiet - sometimes I need it - but I am trying to manage it more responsibly. Others can't read my mind. Quiet with no explanation can be confusing. Quiet with an explanation is healthy and the explaining usually moves me out of the quiet place faster!!

NOTES:

....

....

....

....

....

....

....

....

....

....

....

....

....

....

....

....

....

....

....

LESSON 4

EXPECTATIONS FOR NOTE-TAKING.

DISCUSSION of homework. Spend this class talking about the traits/patterns your students wrote about. Get them engaged and take the next step. After each student shares their homework, ask them the following questions:

1. In describing some of your habitual patterns, can you pinpoint where you learned the habit (mom or dad or older sibling? other?) and **can you notice when you are doing it?** What are the signs?

2. If the habitual pattern doesn't serve you well, **can you recognize the instant the habit appears** and you start falling out of alignment? Share examples of what this feels like and how you notice the falling out of alignment.

3. **What do you want to do instead?** How do you start the process of change?

Because of the topic, it may take some extra effort to get this discussion going, but if you go first, it will help set the tone that while the information may feel personal, we don't have to make it so personal. We can learn to step back and speak more objectively about what we do.....because, after all, we're not the *only* ones who do it. We *all* have our idiosyncrasies. The trick is to recognize them and handle them responsibly.

NOTE ABOUT GRADING HOMEWORK

If it takes more than one day to grade homework, that's alright - it's important to give thoughtful feedback. Given the nature of this course, please think carefully about how you "grade" your students; it's more about supporting/encouraging a growing sense of awareness than right or wrong answers. Be sure graded homework ends up in the Pocket Folder. Remember to make adjustments so this curriculum works for you.

LESSON 5

RETURN GRADED HOMEWORK. Keep in Pocket Folder.

EXPECTATIONS FOR NOTE-TAKING.
Before reading the next chapter, do a quick recap of yesterday. Paying attention to what we do and being able to recognize unhealthy, repetitive patterns allows us to learn and make corrections before an unhealthy pattern firmly takes root in our personality.

READ ALOUD TOGETHER CHAPTER 2, *TOO SOON OLD, TOO LATE SMART*
We are what we do.

POINTS FOR DISCUSSION

1. Happiness is an affirmative state in which our lives have meaning and pleasure; medication isn't enough. We are what we do. (p. 7)

2. Talking vs. Doing: dreams, wishes, promises - pay attention to how you and others actually BEHAVE. Notice the disconnect between words and actions. Past behavior is the most reliable predictor of future behavior. (p. 8)

3. In general, we get not what we deserve, but what we expect. If you expect to be bored, you will be. (p. 8)

4. THREE COMPONENTS OF HAPPINESS: something to do, someone to love, something to look forward to. (p. 9)

5. DEFINING LOVE: we love someone when the importance of his or her needs rises to the level of our own. (p. 9)

6. DEMONSTRATING LOVE: the amount and quality of time we are willing to give the loved one; love is a behavior we do/demonstrate. It's not about promises, it's about actions. (p. 10)

7. When someone says the words you long to hear, don't ignore the incongruent behaviors!!! (p. 11)

8. Love requires the courage to become totally vulnerable to another. (p. 11)

LESSON 5 cont.

9. Somewhere between the extremes of loneliness and self-deception lies our best chance at happiness. (p. 11)

10. We are entitled to receive only that which we are prepared to give. (p. 11)

NOTES:

....

....

....

....

....

....

....

....

....

....

....

....

....

....

....

....

....

LESSON 5 // HOMEWORK

CHAPTER 2 REVISITED

Due tomorrow, extra credit points.

Read Chapter 2 again, this time at home with one of your parents, and talk about it. Be curious, ask questions, learn from their experiences, share some of your own. There is a page in the Journey Workbook for taking notes.

Some suggestions to guide the conversation:

- What gives your life meaning?

- What do you look forward to?

- Are you bored?

- Who do you love and who would you take a bullet for?

- How do you demonstrate love?

- Describe incongruent behaviors (i.e. when words and actions don't line up).

- What are your limitations?

LESSON 5 // HOMEWORK cont.

CHAPTER 2 REVISITED HOMEWORK SAMPLE

Notes from Chapter 2 conversation (extra credit points)

It was fun reading and discussing this chapter with my mom. She raised my brothers and me, and I'm raising my sons, and we both agree that being a mom gives our lives tremendous meaning. Children are a living, dynamic reflection of what we model and teach them, of what we choose to pay attention to, of how we show/express/explain our emotions. I find this wonderfully motivating - I strive to show my best self. After all, you really do get what you give.

We also both agreed that maintaining interests or hobbies is hugely important in avoiding becoming "just one thing." I'm lots of things, I have lots of talents, and I feel really strong and balanced when I'm multi-dimensional. We both messed this up in our marriages - we weren't happily married so we buried ourselves in our kids and mostly shutdown our emotional side. We just did the work and acted like everything was "fine." Bad plan.

Friendships with women add meaning; I cherish the close friends I have. We share our struggles and our joys, and we remind each other that we aren't going crazy!

I look forward to each day. Now, that is. Sunrises, sunsets, exercise. I love planning/taking a trip. I enjoy being a mom. I find joy in simple things - my garden, our farm animals. I'm definitely not bored now.

I'd take a bullet for my sons, my mom and my dad, my brothers.

I demonstrate love by listening, by giving my full attention, by being helpful....I look for ways to be an enabler....I demonstrate love when I talk about or do something thoughtful for someone that reflects my understanding/knowing of them. Smiling. Eye contact. Hugs. Patience. Empathy.

I don't waste much time on incongruent behaviors these days. I notice them rather quickly and come back to alignment and to making sense to myself and others. I don't feel too

LESSON 5 // HOMEWORK cont.

many limitations....just not enough time. Mostly I'm curious, I want to explore what's possible, keep learning and growing, and enjoy every moment.

NOTES:

....

....

....

....

....

....

....

....

....

....

....

....

....

....

....

....

....

....

LESSON 6

EXPECTATIONS FOR NOTE-TAKING.

REVIEW AND CONTINUE DISCUSSION from Lesson 5, points 1-10. Make sure your students have time to take complete notes.

DISCUSSION of homework assignment. How did it go? Was it easy? Awkward? What did you learn about yourself? About your parents?

NOTES:

....

....

....

....

....

....

....

....

....

....

....

....

....

....

....

....

LESSON 7

EXPECTATIONS FOR NOTE-TAKING.

READ ALOUD TOGETHER CHAPTER 3, *TOO SOON OLD, TOO LATE SMART*

It is difficult to remove by logic an idea not placed there by logic in the first place.

POINTS FOR DISCUSSION

1. Stating the obvious - criticism begets anger and unhappiness. Why don't we get this?? Parent-child and spouse-spouse dialogue - how much of it is giving directions or reprimands or criticism? (p. 13)

2. The things we do, the prejudices we hold, and the repetitive conflicts that afflict our lives are seldom the products of rational thought. (p. 13)

3. We are operating on autopilot, trapped in ineffectual life patterns, doing the same thing today that didn't work yesterday. One would think that a process of learning or maturation would cause us to alter our behavior in response to unpleasant consequences, but time and again, we show that this is not true, we don't alter our behavior. (p. 13)

4. THE MOTIVATIONS AND HABIT PATTERNS THAT UNDERLIE MOST OF OUR BEHAVIOR ARE SELDOM LOGICAL; WE ARE MUCH MORE OFTEN DRIVEN BY IMPULSES, PRECONCEPTIONS, AND EMOTIONS OF WHICH WE ARE ONLY DIMLY AWARE. (p. 13)

5. We very often end up living a life that is not the life we imagined.

6. How do we change behavior that is driven by emotions, impulses, and preconceptions?

7. First, we must identify our emotional needs, i.e. to be respected, to be listened to, to feel that we are the center of our partner's life. This is what we mean when we say we want to be loved. (p. 14)

8. How do you satisfy the above-listed emotional needs without offending the person upon whom your happiness depends? You get what you give. If, like most people, you

LESSON 7 cont.

want to be treated with kindness and FORBEARANCE (to be patient or self-controlled when subject to annoyance or provocation), we need to cultivate those qualities in ourselves. (p. 14)

9. The explanation for our present behavior lies in our past experience. (p. 14)

10. Parents often instill an unhealthy sense of obligation in their children to 'make my parents proud.' We should do well in school, stay out of trouble, make a good marriage, and produce grandchildren....and there are many ways parents go about instilling this sense of obligation. (p. 15)

11. By accepting life and nurturance, a child apparently incurs a debt that can be repaid only by meeting parental expectations. Go figure. (p. 15)

12. In fact, OUR CHILDREN OWE US NOTHING. Much is made of the burdens of parenthood: pain of childbirth, loss of sleep, endless driving to activities, the stress of adolescent conflict, the expense of college....and this martyr attitude sets up a sense of obligation. Poorly functioning families that are full of this unhealthy sense of obligation tend to hold on to their children. Well-functioning families tend to let them go. (p. 15-16)

13. We are raising our children to leave us. Obligation-free parenting - what does that look like? Again, watch the dialogue - what do parents do or say to create obligation or guilt?

14. Using logic to overcome maladaptive behaviors usually doesn't work and often runs into the idea that *some ignorance is invincible*. In other words, "PEOPLE CAN BECOME SO WEDDED TO THEIR PARTICULAR VIEW OF HOW THINGS SHOULD WORK THAT THEY IGNORE ALL EVIDENCE THAT SUGGESTS THAT CHANGE IS NECESSARY." (p. 16-17)

LESSON 8

EXPECTATIONS FOR NOTE-TAKING.

REVIEW AND CONTINUE DISCUSSION from Lesson 7, points 1-14.

ACTIVITY: Working in pairs, discuss and make a list of things parents say that create obligation. Be prepared to share with the class.

Examples of creating obligation, a.k.a. guilt-tripping:

"After all I do for you....."
"Is that the best you can do?"
"I spend all day working my butt off so you can....."
"Can't you say thank you?"
"Don't embarrass me."
"Make me proud of you."
"Do you have any idea how much that costs?"
"I'm always cleaning up after you."
"Show me some respect."
"I feel so unappreciated."
"This is the most thankless job."

HOMEWORK
Pay more attention to kindness and obligation.

LESSON 9

EXPECTATIONS FOR NOTE-TAKING.

ANY QUESTIONS about parenting and obligation? Do a quick recap of yesterday's lesson - as much as possible, parent children to leave, debt-free, no strings attached.

READ ALOUD TOGETHER CHAPTER 4, *TOO SOON OLD, TOO LATE SMART*
   The statute of limitations has expired on most of our childhood traumas.

POINTS FOR DISCUSSION

1.   Discuss what the title of this chapter means.

2.   We constantly reinterpret/reweave our personal history in our attempts to explain to ourselves and others how we became the people we are. (p. 18)

3.   We connect childhood experiences to the adult we are today...these experiences shape us and we must learn from them if we are to avoid the repetitious mistakes that make us feel trapped, unhappy, stuck in a long-running drama of our own authorship. It's not just the experiences themselves, but also the meaning we attach to our childhood experiences. (p. 19)

4.   Because accepting responsibility for what we do and how we feel is a choice, it is natural to blame people in our past, particularly parents, for not doing a better job. (p. 19)

5.   Even the most awful experiences do not define our lives forever. (p. 19)

6.   Complaining about how we feel and about the repetitive behaviors that produce familiar and unhappy results is only the beginning..... (p. 20)

7.   Change is the essence of life so, once we're done with the complaining, we must ask: WHAT'S NEXT? (p. 20)

8.   Taking an honest look is a slow, scary, unwieldy process because at the core is the uncomfortable assumption that WE ARE RESPONSIBLE FOR WHAT HAPPENS TO US. (p. 21)

LESSON 9 cont.

9. Good therapy: hold them to the task, listen and make connections between past and present, wonder about underlying motives, express confidence in their ability to come up with solutions that work in their lives. Sit with them while they figure it out. Patient must be convinced therapist is on his/her side. (p. 20-21)

10. Shared qualities of therapy and parenting: patience, empathy, a capacity for affection, and an ability to listen non-judgmentally. (p. 22)

11. Therapists, like parents, are really selling hope. If the patient doesn't bite, the therapist is wasting his/her time. A patient must want to change. (p. 23)

NOTES:

....

....

....

....

....

....

....

....

....

....

....

....

....

LESSON 10

EXPECTATIONS FOR NOTE-TAKING.

REVIEW AND CONTINUE DISCUSSION from Lesson 9, points 1-11.

HOMEWORK

Go to Lesson 10 Homework in the Journey Workbook, explain directions.
Due tomorrow, 50 points.
Use rest of class time to begin.

NOTES:

....

....

....

....

....

....

....

....

....

....

....

....

....

....

....

LESSON 10 // HOMEWORK

CHILDHOOD EXPERIENCES

Due tomorrow, 50 points.

Make a list of 3-5 childhood experiences and then write a paragraph for each experience describing how it could affect you as an adult if left unresolved. These are things you may want to blame your parents for later in life! Remember, I'm looking for quality and depth of thinking - there aren't really right or wrong answers. The paragraphs describing each experience should be at least 5 sentences in length. Be prepared to share your experiences with the class tomorrow. Typed or neat handwriting. As usual, your completed/graded assignment will be kept in your Pocket Folder.

NOTES:

....
....
....
....
....
....
....
....
....
....
....
....
....
....

LESSON 10 // HOMEWORK cont.

CHILDHOOD EXPERIENCES HOMEWORK SAMPLE

1. When I was about 5 years old, I was sliding down the stairs in an apple box. My brother was coming down behind me and when I got stuck many stairs from the bottom, he ran into me and I fell down the rest of the way and broke my collar bone. Now it's mostly just a funny story, but when I saw my sons sliding down our stairs on beanbags, the memory flashed and I was, admittedly, overly concerned that they would get hurt.

2. My parents got divorced when I was about 12 years old and they never really explained why. From my perspective, things didn't look that bad (not knowing how a happy, healthy, loving relationship was supposed to look) so I was confused. This has played out as a desire to know what's going on. I like information and explanations so I've learned how to ask for what I need to know. And I'm teaching my sons to ask questions, ask for what they need to know, and speak up.

3. When I was in 3rd grade, my mom was hospitalized and almost died in surgery. Her mom came to care for us because my dad worked. My mom didn't come home for a month. It was never really explained to me what was going on, what was wrong, when my mom would come home, how serious it was. (As a parent I understand a certain amount of filtering information for kids, but still.) When my mom did get home, she pretty much acted like everything was normal and fine, and this was confusing. So it's important to ask questions to learn what I need to know. And, as a mom, I don't hide health issues from my sons. I just say what it is. Worry and wonder can lead to filling in the blanks the wrong way.

4. When my parents divorced, my dad's message to me was "You don't want to be too complicated and emotions complicate things." I see the point, but at the time, my tweenage interpretation of this led me to be a rational female. Over time, I was pretty much a walking dead person, disregarding emotions when making a decision. There was no joy. I was doing what was "right" or what was expected, but it often didn't feel like what I wanted. I've learned to integrate emotions and how I feel when making decisions - I listen to both my head and my heart. It's pretty easy for this kind of disconnect to sneak up on a person.

LESSON 11

EXPECTATIONS FOR NOTE-TAKING.

CLASS DISCUSSION of homework. Go around the room and have each student share their childhood experiences and discuss how these experiences could play out if left unresolved. Imagine how, years ahead, you might be in conversation with a good friend, a new friend, or potential significant other, getting to know each other, talking about your childhood, and how you might sound like you're still blaming your parents for things you never dealt with.

Discuss how unresolved, possibly red-flag issues can show up in future relationships and affect the foundation of a new relationship, how we often continue playing out repetitive unhealthy patterns until we are in such an unhappy situation that we want it to stop and we want to change how we feel. The longer it goes, the harder it is to change.

Talk about dealing with it vs. sweeping it under the rug vs. downplaying it vs. denying it. The only way to deal with it is to accept responsibility for it, recognize the effect it is having on yourself and others, and have the courage to change the behavior.

Bring the class to a close by reminding students that we always have a choice how closely we want to look at what happens to us and our response to it. Cultivating the desirable attributes of kindness, honesty, courage, responsibility, loyalty, tolerance and humor makes us a much better candidate for healthy relationships. It takes a lot of courage to take an honest look at ourselves.

COLLECT HOMEWORK. Continue the pattern of keeping all homework in the Pocket Folder.

LESSON 12

EXPECTATIONS FOR NOTE-TAKING.

READ ALOUD TOGETHER CHAPTER 5, *TOO SOON OLD, TOO LATE SMART*
   Any relationship is under the control of the person who cares the least.

POINTS FOR DISCUSSION

1. Power struggles about money, children, and sex are often caused by diminished self-respect and unmet expectations. (p. 24)

2. How do we pick someone in the first place? Hindsight shows it is often readiness, lust, and hope rather than a deep knowing of oneself and one another. (p. 25)

3. We often evaluate a person based on education, earning potential, shared interests, trustworthiness, and philosophy of life, which creates a set of expectations. It is the failure of these expectations over time that causes relationships to dissolve. (p. 25)

4. Prenuptial agreements are an ominous development in modern marriage. Have a short debate - are they practical or cynical? How do they affect trust? What is the person trying to protect? Are they a self-fulfilling prophecy? (p. 25)

5. While "no-fault divorce" and "irreconcilable differences" may be enough grounds for divorce these days, needing to find reasons to separate often results in a climate of blame in which each person tries to seize the moral high ground. This is particularly unfortunate when children are involved. (p. 26)

6. As marriages enter the long slide toward alienation, it is seldom a symmetrical process - one person is usually more invested in working things out and not wanting the marriage to end. (p. 26)

7. WHILE IT TAKES TWO PEOPLE TO CREATE A RELATIONSHIP, IT TAKES ONLY ONE TO END IT. (p. 27)

LESSON 12 cont.

HOMEWORK

Think about and be prepared to discuss the behaviors that indicate who cares more or less about a relationship. The following notes are just ideas to help you frame the assignment and tomorrow's class discussion - feel free to add your own ideas.

WHO CARES MORE OR LESS AND HOW CAN YOU TELL?

eye contact

body language

tone of voice

openness, sharing

desire to connect

smiles, laughter

affection

kissing

QUESTIONS TO PONDER......

Does he have time for you? And you him?

Does he really listen? Do you?

Does he follow through on what he says? Do you? (reliable)

Is he kind? Are you? Think of recent/current examples.

Does he know things about you? And you him?

Does he understand you? How does he show it? And vice versa.

Is he generous or selfish? What about you?

Do you feel respected? Do you respect him?

Does he always have to have his way? Do you? (flexibility)

Does he always have the final word? Do you?

What are your conversations about most of the time?

Does he stay put until the conversation is truly over? Do you?

When you get sideways, do you work things out until you both feel better?

What has changed since you first came together?

LESSON 13

EXPECTATIONS FOR NOTE-TAKING.

GO TO Green/Yellow/Red Light in the Journey Workbook.

REVIEW AND CONTINUE DISCUSSION on Lesson 12, points 1-7. Engage the entire class in a conversation about how to recognize who cares more - or less - in a relationship. Take your time with this topic, be thorough, make sure they take good notes, and encourage your students to take the honest look. Use a personal example to get things rolling.

QUESTIONS FOR STEERING THE CONVERSATION:

1. What behaviors and attributes do you want to find because they show caring?
2. What behaviors and attributes are red flags if they show up?
3. Do you engage in any of these undesirable behaviors?
4. Do you recognize them when they show up? and what do you do? Sweep it under the rug? Gloss over it? Apologize? Go silent?
5. What makes us care more - or less - in a relationship? This should lead to a discussion of fear, insecurity, control, expectations.
6. What are we afraid of? What do we expect?
7. The slow slide into alienation.....
8. How do you recognize when parts of you stop showing up? What does that feel and look like? Quiet, avoidance, sarcasm, frustration, sadness, lack of enthusiasm, disinterest, distracted, etc.
9. WHAT TO DO: Catch it early, while the behavior is small and easier to deal with.... because if the behavior pattern goes on too long, it does more damage and only gets harder to deal with and change. Try to get to the root of the behavior, not the superficial reaction itself. What is driving this reaction in you? Where did you learn it and what effect does it have on the other person? It is important not to take everything too personally - step back and look at yourself, be curious about what you do, have compassion for yourself, and a sense of humor always helps! We all struggle. It's like learning to ride a bike - when you fall off, get back on and try again. Practice the skill of being an objective observer of your own self, of not taking yourself too seriously. Own up to how you affect others.

LESSONS 13 cont.

GREEN LIGHT

- kindness
- caring
- consistency
- generosity
- patience
- flexibility
- responsibility
- openness
- respect
- optimism
- courage
- fun

YELLOW LIGHT

- eye contact
- body language
- teeth clenching
- scowling
- eye rolling
- tightness in stomach
- hair pulling
- nail biting
- tone of voice

RED LIGHT

- rude
- selfish
- unpredictable
- sarcastic
- negative
- bullying
- blaming
- condescending
- silence
- gunny-sacking
- public assassination

Green light traits are the ones we want the most- they feel good to both the giver and the receiver. **CULTIVATE THEM.**

Yellow light behaviors are warning signs of disconnect or falling out of alignment, usually in response to a red light trait.

BE BRAVE, DEAL WITH THEM.

Red light traits should make you stop and take a closer look at what's going on. Is there a pattern? **AVOID THEM.**

TAKE AN HONEST LOOK
Which of the above traits/behaviors describe you most of the time????

WATCH OUT!!! SLOW SLIDE INTO ALIENATION - more sarcasm; always busy; disinterested/distracted; lack of intimacy/romance; decreased shared activity/laughter; more time apart; perfunctory; auto pilot; loss of meaning; frustration; impatience; feeling trapped, suffocating; sadness; loneliness.

LESSON 13 cont.

WHAT TO DO.......

1. Catch a pattern early, while it's small.
2. Pay attention to yourself.
3. Know the difference between feeling open and closed.
4. As soon as you recognize you're shutting down, say to yourself "STOP" or "I feel myself shutting down" or "This doesn't feel right" or "Don't do the same old thing" or whatever words work for you.....

TO CREATE A PAUSE......

5. In the pause, identify what you're feeling and what caused it, and explain what you want to do instead - the new behavior that will serve you better.
6. Do the new behavior. Catch yourself every time you start to feel or do one of the red or yellow light behaviors. Do your best and keep trying. It takes practice and pretty soon the new behavior will replace the old behavior.....and even if the old behavior never goes away completely (we're only human!), you'll be more skilled at dealing with it effectively.

UPSHOT
More green light behaviors - compassion, empathy, self-awareness......more connection to self/others.....more meaning, more fun!
MORE OF THE GOOD STUFF!

LESSON 14

EXPECTATIONS FOR NOTE-TAKING.
Use this class to step back and catch your breath.

FINISH YESTERDAY'S DISCUSSION about recognizing desirable and undesirable attributes and recognizing the behaviors that indicate we are shutting down.
In particular, reinforce the steps we can take to create a pause so we become less reactive and more authentically responsive, so we can integrate our feelings with our behavior in a mature way. Share a personal example if you want. Lots of important ideas here. Answer any questions.

GO TO EMOTIONAL MENU PROJECT (EMP) description in the Journey Workbook. Pick a due date two weeks out and have them fill it in at the top. Review the assignment and show the example you have made. Brainstorm ideas with them, answer questions, pass out the construction paper. Announce that there will be a progress check in one week.

GO TO JOURNEY CHECKLIST #1 in the Journey Workbook and review. Clarify the expectations for a complete, organized workbook and folder.

HOMEWORK
Begin thinking about your EMP.
Prepare your Journey Workbook for tomorrow's check, 50 points.

LESSON 14 // PROJECT

EMOTIONAL MENU

Due in two weeks, 100 points. ————————————

MATERIALS: construction paper, colored pencils or markers

This project is an exercise in taking an honest look at yourself, specifically some themes of your personality. Using the format of a restaurant menu, you will design the cover of your menu, you will write a bit of history about your 'restaurant,' and you will describe at least five different 'dishes' you 'serve' at your 'restaurant.' (Check out the sample.)

- The cover of your menu should reflect who you are - your interests and hobbies, your passions, the things that make you tick.

- Of course your restaurant needs a name!

- The bit of history should summarize your philosophy about the 'food' you serve; that is, how do you think you show up on the planet? What are you about? What is your purpose? Stay in the metaphor.

- On the inside, name and describe at least 5 dishes that represent some of your personality traits. For example, something you love to eat, like Home-made Chicken Noodle Soup, might be you at your best, while something really hot, like Kung Pao Chicken, is you when you're angry.

- Describe how you 'do' the trait/dish - that is, what you look like when you're happy or angry or frustrated, etc., and what helps you stay in that trait (if it's healthy) and what helps move you out of it (if it's unhealthy).

Creativity, depth of thinking, neatness, proper GUM (Grammar, Usage, Mechanics), following directions - it all counts. Some computer use is okay. Have fun with it!

dining with Robin at the

NAMASTE CAFE

SAMPLE MENU COVER

Pasta with Spring Vegetables

My favorite place to be... everything is humming, I'm all lined up - my thinking flows with my emotions, there's a spring in my step and a smile in my eyes, on my face, and in my voice. I feel kind, loving, patient, cuddly, and affectionate. Strong and clear, confident and determined. Irrepressible. I'm easy to be around. FUN. Playful. Light. All the best parts are showing up and blending together.
PEACEFUL.

Citrus-Roasted Salmon

Sour is not a favorite flavor and is usually short-lived. I'm fussy and out of sorts, but not full-on angry... frustrated, impatient, possible clipped words, distracted. I'm listening but not fully present. Usually I just need some time to think things through- writing helps- or exercise- and calm everything down. Try cleaning house. Get busy. Do I need sleep?

Walnut-Crusted Chicken

Strong flavor. I'm on it. I feel strong physically, salty with sweat, I feel alive... maybe there's a feisty piece, a bit of bad-ass attitude. There's also a maturity and wisdom ingredient... a bit of the teacher shows up and my understanding of human nature. This is me being energetic, upbeat, sporty, compassionate... and full of HOPE. It's a very solid, grounding feeling.

Steak with Spicy Papaya-Carrot Salsa

Watch out! I'm ANGRY and I might raise my voice and I might even swear. I won't like being interrupted. I need to just feel the anger and vent it. It will spin itself out and I'll be able to think again. I will stay mindful of how I express my anger so I don't say irretrievably hurtful things, and I will never physically hurt anyone. I know that holding on to anger will do a bad thing.

Banana-Strawberry-Blueberry-OJ-Honey-Vanilla Yogurt Smoothie

smooth
easy
open
relaxed
FRESH!!!

Berry Grunt

I don't like this place...I feel alone and disconnected from myself and others. I'm quiet, not very talkative, not available... sometimes I sound tight, edgy, brittle. I go to this place when I've been hurt or misunderstood. Please be patient. A hug sometimes works to bring me around, soften my hard edges. Eventually I'll be able to explain why I got stuck and I'll reconnect.

SAMPLE MENU

Established October 10, 1963

Hard to believe that I've been in business over 45 years now. Eating nutritious, delicious food has always been a priority for me because I've always led an active, athletic, outdoorsy lifestyle. Being fit is a top priority. Yeah, I've served up and eaten my share of both tasteless food and junk food, and - not surprisingly - it rarely did a good thing.

When I underwent an extreme life make-over awhile back, one of the upshots was that preparing and sharing consciously healthy food has taken on a whole new meaning. I appreciate the texture, depth, and variety of flavors in a way I never experienced before. I celebrate how colorful farm-fresh fruits and vegetables are. I slow down and actually TASTE my food instead of mindlessly forking through it. I'm adventurous and enjoy using new ingredients in different ways... and know when to stir up a tried-and-true, comforting favorite.

Healthy food doesn't just nourish and fuel our bodies - it feeds the heart and soul too.

Open 24/7/365

ENJOY

Robin

SAMPLE MENU HISTORY

LESSON 14 // JOURNEY CHECKLIST #1

- **TITLE PAGE** (optional student artwork): PURSUIT OF HAPPINESS

- **LESSON 1** Homework - Three Questions

- **LESSONS 2 & 3** Notes and Reflections on Chapter 1

- **LESSON 3** Homework - Personality Traits

- **LESSON 4** Notes, habits and patterns

- **LESSONS 5 & 6** Notes and Reflections on Chapter 2

- **LESSONS 7 & 8** Notes and Reflections on Chapter 3; Creating obligation

- **LESSONS 9 & 10** Notes and Reflections on Chapter 4

- **LESSON 10** Homework - Childhood Experiences

- **LESSONS 12 & 13** Notes and Reflections on Chapter 5; Who cares more/less

- **LESSON 13** Green/Yellow/Red Light

- **LESSON 14** EMOTIONAL MENU PROJECT Description and ideas

INITIAL/DATE COMPLETE _____/_____

POINTS OUT OF 50_____

LESSON 15

JOURNEY WORKBOOK CHECK. Have them work in pairs and complete the check. Walk around the room with your grade book, spot check, and assign points out of 50 possible.

EXPECTATIONS FOR NOTE-TAKING.

READ ALOUD TOGETHER CHAPTER 6, *TOO SOON OLD, TOO LATE SMART*
Feelings follow behavior.

POINTS FOR DISCUSSION

1. In therapy, people want to change the way they feel - they want relief, a return to normalcy, to feel better....their lives have an unremitting seriousness, they have lost their capacity to laugh and have fun. (p. 28)

2. WE DO NOT CONTROL HOW WE FEEL OR WHAT WE THINK - efforts to control feelings and thoughts usually only exacerbate them. (p. 29)

3. Our lives have taught us that certain behaviors predictably bring pleasure and satisfaction. (p. 29)

4. When we're 'unmotivated,' we stop doing the things that bring us pleasure and satisfaction, and disconnect from the fact that doing these very things will break the stalemate caused by inaction and its associated feelings of meaninglessness and despair. Get busy and we'll start to feel better!!! (p. 29)

5. Courage and determination are mandatory if you want to change. Ask: what are you saving yourself for? (p. 30)

6. Genuine mental illness vs. behavioral disorders - when is medication necessary and when is it an excuse to avoid responsibility?

7. When you're depressed, the implication is that through no fault of your own you have lost control of your life and need time to heal....and, so, little is expected of you, which can be a counterproductive approach. (p. 30)

LESSON 15 cont.

8. Example - ADD, Attention Deficit Disorder. Disorganized, daydreaming procrastinators now have a medical explanation for their inattention and an effective treatment: stimulant drugs. Their spirits are better and they get more done when taking an amphetamine....who wouldn't?! (p. 33)

9. The problem with all these diagnoses that can label you "disabled," which are basically descriptions of certain behavioral patterns, is that they can remove the sense of responsibility for overcoming one's problems. (p. 34)

10. Compensating people who feel helpless validates the emotion and insures that it persists, and creates an incentive to surrender autonomy and a sense of competence - it undermines self-esteem. (p. 34)

11. PEOPLE HAVE AN OBLIGATION TO ALTER THEIR BEHAVIOR IN WAYS THAT ALLOW THEM TO EXERT GREATER CONTROL OVER THEIR LIVES....WHICH FUELS SELF-ESTEEM. FEELINGS FOLLOW BEHAVIOR. (p. 35)

12. Discuss the "fine line between expressing empathy and solidarity for those who suffer vs. endorsing a passive dependency." (p. 35)

HOMEWORK

Continued work on the EMP.

HINT: There might be a pop quiz coming soon......points for discussion/class notes are a good source of review material.......

LESSON 16

EXPECTATIONS FOR NOTE-TAKING.

REVIEW AND CONTINUE DISCUSSION from Lesson 15, points 1-12. The point here is that, barring real mental illness, people have an obligation and responsibility to change their behavior in ways that allow them to exert greater control over their lives. If we're feeling depressed, changing what we're doing is the antidote, not stagnating in inactivity. We are not helpless. We don't need excuses. We don't necessarily need a pill. We need courage and determination to keep our lives heading in a good, productive direction. On the board or an overhead projector, **CREATE A FLOW CHART** depicting how this slide into stagnation/depression works (see Lesson 16 in the Journey Workbook and sample on next page). Next to the step about getting busy, have them share - and write down - activities they know are always enjoyable and help them feel better. (This will come in handy for a project later on in the course.)

HOMEWORK

Continued work on the EMP....and don't forget about that possible "pop" quiz......

NOTES:

....

....

....

....

....

....

....

....

....

....

....

LESSON 16 cont.

FEELINGS FOLLOW BEHAVIOR

↓

Life is too serious. No fun. No laughter.

↓

Feel bad. Unmotivated. Want relief!

↙   ↘

Stop doing fun things. "Waiting" for motivation.

↘   ↙

Can be a VERY LONG wait.

↓

Stalemate, doldrums, depression.

↓

Don't take a pill - get busy! get moving! do the things you
enjoy! (i.e. change your behavior)

↓

Start to feel better. Motivated again. More fun. Laughter
comes back. Self-esteem improves.

↓

FEELINGS FOLLOW BEHAVIOR

LESSON 17

Today the class takes their first pop quiz.

PASS OUT THE POP QUIZ on chapters 1-6, briefly explain the expectations for answering the questions, answer any of your students questions, and remind them to use complete sentences, proper spelling, and correct grammar.

PAY ATTENTION. If everyone finishes the quiz and there is class time left, go over the quiz together. Those who finish early can...

READ CHAPTER 7, *TOO SOON OLD, TOO LATE SMART*

Be bold and mighty forces will come to your aid.

COLLECT THE POP QUIZZES for grading and to be returned tomorrow. Graded pop quizzes will be filed in the Pocket Folder.

HOMEWORK

Continued work on the EMP.

NOTES:

....

....

....

....

....

....

....

....

....

....

....

LESSON 17 // POP QUIZ

POP QUIZ #1 ON CHAPTERS 1-6

50 points

Answer the following questions to the best of your ability. Proper grammar and spelling count. Write on the back, if needed.

1. Define 'happiness' and include its three components.

2. Define 'personality.'

3. What are we trying to accomplish when we construct our maps of the world?

4. Where do we find the explanation for our behavior?

5. Describe 'obligation-free parenting.'

6. What are the shared qualities of parenting and therapy? What are parents and therapists really selling?

7. List 5 undesirable attributes of people to avoid. What desirable attribute governs all the others?

8. What is the only consolation for the pain of trial and error learning?

9. What happens to us when we're depressed and unmotivated?

10. Explain the idea that 'feelings follow behavior'.

LESSON 17 // POP QUIZ cont.

POP QUIZ #1 SAMPLE ANSWER KEY

1. Happiness is a positive state in which our lives have meaning. Its components are something to do, someone to love, and something to look forward to.

2. Personality is habitual ways of thinking, feeling, and relating to others.

3. Aside from assisting us in making sense of our life, we strive to construct a map that allows us to avoid people who are not worthy of our time and trust, and to cherish those who are.

4. The explanation for our behavior lies in our past experience.

5. "Obligation-free parenting" is parenting without any expectation that your children owe you something. No strings attached.

6. Parenting and therapy share the qualities of patience, empathy, a capacity for affection, and an ability to listen non-judgmentally. We sit with our kids while they figure things out about themselves and their lives. Parents and therapists are really selling hope.

7. Selfish, rude/sarcastic, dishonest, unreliable, negative, bullying/blaming/mean, arrogant, etc. Kindness is the desirable attribute that governs all others.

8. The only consolation for the pain is the opportunity to learn and get it right the next time.

9. When we're depressed and unmotivated, we stop doing the things that bring us pleasure so we become even more depressed and unmotivated. We withdraw from life.

10. When we're depressed, we withdraw from life, people, and activities. But if we can get ourselves motivated, moving, and doing things we know we enjoy, we will gradually start to feel better. Happiness is an activity, something you do, and the feeling of enjoying doing it.

OVERVIEW

LESSONS 18-30

TOO SOON OLD, TOO LATE SMART CHAPTERS

7 Be bold, and mighty forces will come to your aid.

8 The perfect is the enemy of the good.

9 Life's two most important questions are "Why?" and "Why not?" The trick is to know which one to ask.

10 Our greatest strengths are our greatest weaknesses.

11 The most secure prisons are those we construct for ourselves.

12 The problems of the elderly are frequently serious but seldom interesting.

HOMEWORK ASSIGNMENTS (2) + samples

- Personal Ad
- When I'm Old

GUEST SPEAKER OPTION

POP QUIZ #2 ON CHAPTERS 7-12

LESSON 18

RETURN GRADED POP QUIZZES. Go over any questions. Keep in Pocket Folder.

EXPECTATIONS - LISTEN AND PARTICIPATE.

READ ALOUD TOGETHER CHAPTER 7, *TOO SOON OLD, TOO LATE SMART*
Be bold, and mighty forces will come to your aid.

In this chapter, the author changes direction a bit and talks about his experience in the Vietnam War. Dr. Livingston wrote and passed out "The Blackhorse Prayer" to the guests at a change-of-command ceremony for General Patton, with the upshot being that he was arrested. Years later he returned to the site where he was 'reborn.'

After reading the chapter aloud with your students, walk into a discussion about moral courage and taking a stand for what you believe is right. Perhaps a current event would serve as an example. Discuss what prevents us from taking a stand (fear, doubt, might get in trouble) and what motivates us to draw the line (anger/frustration, right vs. wrong). Have students share a current/recent example from their own lives, an experience where they faced a difficult choice, and what it's like to struggle with making an unpopular choice. Discuss the potential fall-out. Discuss strategies for staying steady and getting through it. What did the author mean by being 'reborn?'

HOMEWORK
Continued work on the EMP.

LESSON 19

EXPECTATIONS FOR NOTE-TAKING AND PARTICIPATION.

READ ALOUD TOGETHER CHAPTER 8, *TOO SOON OLD, TOO LATE SMART*

The perfect is the enemy of the good.

POINTS FOR DISCUSSION

1. There is a kind of track we are put on early in life with the implicit suggestion that, if we "succeed," we will be happy and secure. (p. 41)

2. Education is the primary means to this end - where you go to school, i.e. college, speaks to social standing and your potential for success. (p. 41-42)

3. Hopefully we learn a set of skills that people pay us for so we can accumulate the things that supposedly make us happy; so we become "full members in a society that guarantees to its citizens the pursuit of happiness." (p. 42)

4. We are also taught that it is important to form intimate relationships - for access to sex, to parent, for financial stability, and emotional security. (p. 42)

5. We are given quite a bit of direction about obtaining economic success, but we are not given much direction when it comes to how to relate to others. While, theoretically, the needs and desires of the opposite sex are complementary to our own, the needs and desires remain frustratingly obscure. (p. 42)

6. Problem: while we are largely in control of getting educated and choosing a career that will enable us to "succeed," exerting control in our intimate relationships is disastrous - it doesn't work because it becomes getting what you want at the expense of someone else and there's no chance of achieving intimacy. (p. 42-43)

7. Control vs. perfection. If we bend the world and the people in it to our will, we lose the need to negotiate differences, to endure the uncertainty of failure and rejection; we use power and manipulation to get what we want and lose touch with the person on the other side of the interaction. (p. 43)

LESSON 19 cont.

8. Perfectionistic people tend to be demanding of themselves and those around them; they tend to manifest an obsessive orderliness that is alienating; they do not trust feelings and prefer to occupy themselves with things they can count. (p. 43)

9. A certain amount of perfectionism is good. Discuss examples - heart surgeon, auto or airplane mechanic....

10. THE PARADOX OF PERFECTION: in some settings, like work, being a perfectionist is effective, but in other settings, notably IN OUR INTIMATE RELATIONSHIPS, WE GAIN CONTROL ONLY BY RELINQUISHING IT. (p. 44)

DISCUSS what their tracks - education and relationship - look like and where they're getting directions.

HOMEWORK

Continued work on the EMP.

NOTES:

....
....
....
....
....
....
....
....
....
....
....
....

LESSON 20

EXPECTATIONS FOR NOTE-TAKING.

ANNOUNCEMENT: There will be a progress check on the EMP tomorrow. Bring it to class, show what you've done so far and what you have planned. The assignment is due in a week.

REVIEW AND CONTINUE DISCUSSION from Lesson 19, points 1-10. The gist of this lesson is that what works in one area of your life - taking charge of your education and being successful at work - may not work well in another area of your life. Control does not cultivate intimacy in relationships - in fact, it does a bad thing. Strive to be versatile and wear more than one hat, and learn to move smoothly between the various hats you wear - student, friend, child, sibling, co-worker, volunteer, etc. Be sure students have time to take good notes.

HOMEWORK

Continued work on the EMP and bring it to class tomorrow for the progress check.

......Be mindful of kindness.

LESSON 21

EXPECTATIONS FOR NOTE-TAKING.

PROGRESS CHECK EMPs. Give feedback, offer suggestions, answer questions.

READ ALOUD TOGETHER CHAPTER 9, *TOO SOON OLD, TOO LATE SMART*
> Life's two most important questions are "Why?" and "Why not?"
> The trick is knowing which one to ask.

POINTS FOR DISCUSSION

1. If we want to change ourselves, we must first understand why we do things, especially repetitive behavior patterns that don't serve us well. The reasons for what we do and how we live are often obscure. (p. 45)

2. "The unexamined life is not worth living" but it is hard work and potentially embarrassing to take an honest look at what we do. (p. 45)

3. Freud's greatest contribution - the theory of the unconscious mind: what is going on just below the level of our awareness that influences our behavior. "Freudian slips." (p. 46)

4. Acknowledging that repressed desires, resentments, and motivations exist below our level of consciousness and affect our day-to-day behavior is an important step toward self-understanding. (p. 46)

5. Ignoring the existence of our subconscious tends to create problems. One consequence is destructive patterns of behavior and being surprised that we keep making the same mistake. Rather than recognize the pattern, we prefer to call it coincidence or blame someone else. We avoid asking "why?" does this keep happening. (p. 46-47)

6. We also have trouble asking "why not?" because it implies risk and change, and most of us are afraid of change. We are steeped in our habits, we live largely risk-averse lives, we stop testing ourselves. You'd think our fears would back off with age but this is often not the case - we grow even more invested in protecting ourselves. (p. 47)

7. Example: finding a partner in middle age. Internet dating. Requires confidence. Endless

LESSON 21 cont.

excuses. Many choose loneliness. Instead of asking "why not?" to the new opportunity, we defend ourselves from disappointment/rejection and instead ask "why?" (p. 47-48)

8. Leading a "safe" life can cut off our spirit of adventure. We're like a pop that lost its fizz. Keep going for it!!

9. Learning how to love - the highest stakes are when we're talking about our heart. How and where do we learn this? If you try to love someone, you risk being hurt, rejected, etc. and if you don't try, you are guaranteed to be alone. So how do we balance the risk of making mistakes against the certainty of aloneness if we play it safe? (p. 49)

10. In the game of love, both sides are supposed to win, it's not a competition. But how do we know the other person shares this cooperative vision? (There's a balance between being cynical and a fool.) We have to keep getting to know people, keep dating, keep taking the risk and putting ourselves out there. (p. 49)

11. Anytime you learn something new, there's a learning curve, it takes time, you make sometimes-painful mistakes - the same is true with our hearts. Along the way to finding someone worthy to love, you are going to get hurt, you are going to make some mistakes - this shouldn't come as a surprise. However, it's nothing like the despair of being alone. (p. 49)

12. To love requires taking risks and is an act of courage. To refuse to take the risks, to protect our hearts against all loss, is an act of despair. (p. 49)

HOMEWORK

EMP should be close to finished.

If you remember, ask your parents if they ever made a "Freudian slip" and have them tell the story.

LESSON 22

EXPECTATIONS FOR NOTE-TAKING.

REVIEW AND CONTINUE DISCUSSION on Lesson 21, points 1-12. The key in this lesson is to make sure your students understand when to ask the important questions "why?" and "why not?"

When it comes to destructive patterns of behavior, the question to ask is "why?" and then not be afraid to look below the surface at the subconscious mind and make changes. For example, why do I keep dating this person I don't feel comfortable with?

When it comes to trying something new, like dating in middle age, the operative question is "why not?" and then be open to new experiences in spite of the risks. Talk about the concept of beginner's mind and how it's an attitude that keeps us youthful and open.

Also remind them that learning to love has a learning curve like any new skill or activity. Don't be surprised when you make mistakes or get hurt - therein lies the opportunity to keep cultivating (in yourself) and getting better at recognizing (in others) the person who understands that love is a cooperative vision in which both sides are supposed to win.

ASK YOUR STUDENTS: What happened the first time you learned to walk or ride a bike or read or ski? How did you learn? What new thing have you tried lately?

HOMEWORK
Finish up the EMP. It is due in two days.

LESSON 23

EXPECTATIONS FOR NOTE-TAKING.

READ ALOUD TOGETHER CHAPTER 10, *TOO SOON OLD, TOO LATE SMART*

> Our greatest strengths are our greatest weaknesses.

POINTS FOR DISCUSSION

1. Certain personality traits that are tied to academic and professional success - dedication to work, attention to detail, ability to manage time, conscientiousness - can be difficult to live with. (p. 50)

2. Keeping lists, perfectionistic attitudes, devotion to effort over pleasure and friendships, lack of flexibility, and stubbornness tend to go against closeness, relaxation, and tolerance. (p. 51)

3. We have different roles - worker, partner, friend, parent - and different roles have different attitudes....so we need to be able to switch gears and match the attitude with the role. (p. 51)

4. Be careful of being drawn to someone who has complementary needs - "serious man needs fun woman" - and how this can lead to disappointment and frustration over time.

5. Compulsive people are vulnerable to depression, as is anyone who seeks perfection in an imperfect world. Again, approaches that make them successful at work often don't work in relationships. When their sense of being in charge is threatened, they often redouble the behaviors that created the problem in the first place...and the resulting conflict produces more frustration and discouragement, which reinforces the sense of failure. So pay attention to those behaviors listed above in #2. (p. 52)

6. "How's that working?" is a good question to ask because it focuses on the pragmatic and practical instead of challenging someone's deeply held convictions. Avoid making it personal; e.g. "Why would you do that?" or "What were you thinking?" are not-so-good questions to ask. (p. 52)

7. Moderation in all human characteristics; extremes can produce undesirable results. (p. 53)

LESSON 23 cont.

8. The things we are sure will make us happy seldom do. (p. 53)

9. Paradoxes: the pursuit of pleasure brings pain; the greatest risk is not taking any; everything in life is a good news/bad news story; our dream vacation put us in debt; youth is wasted on the young, etc. (p. 53)

10. The role of impermanence: all our efforts to learn, to acquire, to hold on to what we have, eventually come to naught. (p. 53-54)

11. Only by embracing mortality can we be happy in the time we have. (p. 54)

HOMEWORK

Finish the EMP.

Due tomorrow, 100 points.

NOTES:

....

....

....

....

....

....

....

....

....

....

....

....

....

LESSON 24

EXPECTATIONS FOR NOTE-TAKING, EMP ready to be turned in.

REVIEW AND CONTINUE DISCUSSION on Lesson 23, points 1-11. Reinforce the point that sometimes our greatest strengths that allow us to be successful in work can be problematic in our personal relationships. Moderation in all human attributes, instead of extremes, tends to offer the best results.

COLLECT EMPs and explain that they will be shared in class tomorrow along with their Personal Ads.

HOMEWORK

Go to Lesson 24 Homework in the Journey Workbook, explain directions.

Due tomorrow, 50 points.

Use available class time to begin.

NOTES:

....

....

....

....

....

....

....

....

....

....

....

....

....

LESSON 24 // HOMEWORK

PERSONAL AD

Due tomorrow, 50 points.

In approximately 50 words, write a personal ad describing yourself and the type of person you would like to meet. Be prepared to share your homework in class tomorrow.

NOTES:

....

....

....

....

....

....

....

....

....

....

....

....

....

....

....

....

....

LESSON 24 // HOMEWORK cont.

PERSONAL AD HOMEWORK SAMPLE

Fun-loving, attractive, athletic, well-educated 45 yo woman who is awake and open seeks kind, reliable, tall, handsome, fit man who knows how to work and play. Must stay put when things get sideways. Must be willing to enjoy two young (10 and 13), loving boys. Must enjoy travel to warm places. No smoking. Yes laughing, reading, listening to music, realizing dreams, being outside, enjoying the moment.

NOTES:

....
....
....
....
....
....
....
....
....
....
....
....
....
....
....
....
....

LESSON 25

EXPECTATIONS: some note-taking; class participation.

GIVE STUDENTS AN OPTION: share either their EMP or their Personal Ad. Depending on your class size, you might not have time for each student to share both of these assignments so give them a choice. Take willing volunteers - you may need to go first so be prepared. Remind students to be kind and supportive of each other as they present. Again, here is where an ability to step back from yourself and maintain a sense of humor is important.

If a student chooses to share their Personal Ad, guide them in a discussion of what style the student might attract with their ad and how this might play out over time, the pros and cons of "like attracts like" and "opposites attract." Opposites may attract but do they remain attracted to each other? What things are important to have in common? For example, eating/exercise habits, sleep patterns (night owl vs. early bird), personal hygiene, is the person neat or sloppy?

At the end of class, make sure you have each student's Menu and Personal Ad for grading and additional comments (see EMP Guidelines for Grading sheet). Make thoughtful comments when "grading." Be mindful of your example and the message you want to send, namely kindness.

REMEMBER: All graded homework gets filed in the Pocket Folder.

LESSON 25 cont.

EMOTIONAL MENU PROJECT

Guidelines for Grading

10 points	followed directions	_____
10 points	neatness	_____
10 points	proper GUM	_____
30 points	creativity	_____
40 points	depth of thinking/content	_____

                 TOTAL   _____

ADDITIONAL COMMENTS:

....

....

....

....

....

....

....

....

....

....

....

....

....

LESSON 26

EXPECTATIONS FOR NOTE-TAKING.

FINISH UP from yesterday - any more EMPs/Personal Ads to share?

READ ALOUD TOGETHER CHAPTER 11, *TOO SOON OLD, TOO LATE SMART*
    The most secure prisons are those we construct for ourselves.

POINTS FOR DISCUSSION

1. We often don't think of it as a loss of freedom, but we voluntarily impose constraints upon our lives - things we are afraid to try, unfulfilled dreams - we place limitations on what we can become. (p. 55)

2. Usually it is fear and anxiety that keep us from doing the things that would make us happy - educate ourselves, be successful in our work, fall in love. We break a lot of promises to ourselves and often don't do what is necessary to become the people we want to be. (p. 55-56)

3. Naturally we like to shift blame for our failures - parents, lack of opportunity, not enough time, have to make a living - but really, keeping our expectations low protects us from disappointment. Also, many of us are doing the same thing today as yesterday - and last year; we are on autopilot. (p. 56)

4. We do not like to think of ourselves as being trapped, and we tend to be impatient, so where do we find the determination and patience required to achieve the things we want? (p. 56)

5. BEFORE WE CAN DO ANYTHING, WE MUST BE ABLE TO IMAGINE IT. Sounds easy but many people don't make the connection between behavior and feelings...and we have become used to the idea that much of what we don't like about ourselves and our lives can be 'fixed' quickly and with little effort on our part (mood-lifting medication, plastic surgery, self-improvement through consumption). (p. 57)

6. Happiness cannot be bought.

LESSON 26 cont.

7. Know the difference between an expression of intent and simply a wish; the latter is not reality. (p. 58)

8. Change is incremental and takes time. You must be ready and willing to exercise the fortitude required to examine your life, take responsibility for your feelings, and decide what you need to do to be happy - and then do it. (p. 58-59)

9. Confession may be good for the soul, but unless it is accompanied by altered behavior, it remains only words in the air. (p. 59)

10. THE ONLY COMMUNICATION THAT CAN BE TRUSTED IS BEHAVIOR. It is our actions that truly define us. (p. 60)

11. "I love you" is one of the most confusing things we tell each other. We long to hear this reassuring message, but if the words are unsupported by consistently loving behavior, it's a lie....a promise unlikely to be fulfilled. (p. 60)

12. The disconnect between what we say and what we do is not just a measure of hypocrisy; it also shows that we pay too much attention to the words and not enough to the actions that really define us. (p. 60)

HOMEWORK

Give some thought to or engage in a conversation with one of your parents about the constraints we impose on ourselves. What walls are you building around yourself for protection and to avoid disappointment? Do you make statements of intent or just wishful thinking? Is there a disconnect between what you say and what you do? Be prepared to discuss in class.

LESSON 26 // HOMEWORK

SELF-IMPOSED CONSTRAINTS HOMEWORK SAMPLE

Notes from Chapter 11 (extra credit points)

Self-imposed constraints - am I breaking promises to myself???

PHYSICAL CHALLENGE - running the Ridge Run, keep doing yoga, stay in shape!! Don't get lazy and, really, draw the line at buying a bigger size pants!!!

WRITING A BOOK - I've been thinking and talking about this for the longest time. I have started a book, I'm about 10,000 words along, but have stopped writing it for now. Instead I'm doing this project - creating a curriculum for a practical, important class to teach high school students. It's very satisfying and challenging.

BEING A MOM - I'm staying true to my desire to be available to my kids. I'm able to do my work around being a mom and I'm lucky for that. Pretty soon they'll be off on their own.

MARRIAGE - I told myself plenty of "lies" during my marriage. I didn't really understand what was happening and the things that were wrong.....so I was breaking a promise to myself about the importance of being happy. I got help, figured it out, got divorced. Who knows what's next?

TRAVEL - This is something I really enjoy, and if we aren't getting out and doing some trips, it's often because it's "easier" to stay home and there's always "so much work" to do. The work can wait - go have an adventure!

For the most part, my statements of intent line up with my actions - sometimes it takes time, but I do what I say I'm going to do.....and that's a strong, clear place to be. Integrity.

LESSON 27

EXPECTATIONS FOR NOTE-TAKING.

REVIEW AND CONTINUE DISCUSSION on Lesson 26, points 1-12. Students should have an increased awareness of self-imposed constraints and how this can lead to feeling trapped, and how we can change how we feel if we are willing to do the work to change our behavior. Talk is cheap, as they say - pay attention to behavior because it is our actions that truly define us.

ASK how many students talked to a parent about this topic. Discuss the sorts of walls we build around ourselves to keep expectations low and avoid disappointment. Is there a disconnect between what you say and what you do? Are you a dreamer or a doer?

DROP A HINT... There might be a pop quiz coming in the near future.......

NOTES:

....

....

....

....

....

....

....

....

....

....

....

....

....

LESSON 28

EXPECTATIONS FOR NOTE-TAKING.

READ ALOUD TOGETHER CHAPTER 12, *TOO SOON OLD, TOO LATE SMART*
The problems of the elderly are frequently serious but seldom interesting.

POINTS FOR DISCUSSION

1. Old age is commonly seen as a time of entitlement, but really, the elderly are devalued and we slide into thinking that old people don't have anything useful to contribute to society. (p. 61)

2. We isolate the old in their own institutions and communities, which reflects 1.) the belief that they have little to teach us, and 2.) a desire to decrease our interactions with them. (p. 62)

3. And look at what we do to delay our own demise! $150 billion dollars a year spent in the cosmetics industry to fight hair loss and wrinkles. (p. 62)

4. Cosmic joke: we are the only species able to contemplate our own death. (p. 62-63)

5. So the old get angry at being marginalized and devalued by society...and so they resort to complaining....and this doesn't set the best example for those of us coming next...and it is discouraging to be around....so taking care of old people feels like a burden. (p. 63)

6. Most old people are preoccupied with self-centered complaints. This preoccupation, unpleasant to be around, leads to virtually no contact with the young and a void of intellectual stimulation that can sometimes delay the onset of dementia. (p. 64-65)

7. PARENTHOOD, A VOLUNTARY COMMITMENT, DOES NOT INCUR A RECIPROCAL OBLIGATION IN THE YOUNG, EITHER TO CONFORM THEIR LIVES TO OUR PARENTAL PREFERENCES OR TO LISTEN ENDLESSLY TO OUR PROTESTS ABOUT THE RAVAGES OF TIME. (p. 65-66)

8. The old have a duty to suffer the losses of age with as much grace and determination

LESSON 28 cont.

as they can muster, and to avoid inflicting their discomforts on those who love them. (p. 66)

9. A primary task of parents throughout their lives is to convey to the young a sense of optimism - the greatest gift that can pass from one generation to the next is the conviction that we can achieve happiness amidst the losses and uncertainties that life contains. (p. 66)

10. LIKE ALL THE VALUES WE WISH TO TEACH OUR CHILDREN - honesty, commitment, empathy, respect, hard work - THE SUPREME IMPORTANCE OF HOPE IS TAUGHT BY EXAMPLE. (p. 66)

11. Imagine feeling invisible, like you have nothing useful to say, becoming the object of obligatory visits, of not being listened to...all very painful experiences, but don't inflict the young with boring conversation as retaliation for feeling devalued and irrelevant. (p. 66)

12. Our ability to contemplate our imminent mortality gives us the opportunity to be brave. Retaining a sense of humor and interest in others as the curtain closes is a gift to those who survive us - it fulfills our final obligation to them and expresses our gratitude for the gift of life that we have enjoyed for so long. (p. 66)

HOMEWORK

Go to Lesson 28 Homework in the Journey Workbook, explain directions.
Due tomorrow, 50 points.

LESSON 28 // HOMEWORK

WHEN I'M OLD

Due tomorrow, 50 points.

Think about and/or talk with your parents about mortality and the old people (especially grandparents) in your life.

- Where are they?
- What are they doing?
- What is your connection to each other?

Write a paragraph, about 100 words, describing how you want to be and show up when you are old.

NOTES:

....

....

....

....

....

....

....

....

....

....

....

....

....

....

LESSON 28 // HOMEWORK cont.

WHEN I'M OLD HOMEWORK SAMPLE

When I'm old, I hope to be mentally sharp. I hope to do yoga when I'm 80! I hope to be hiking still. I hope to be around people. I hope to enjoy my children and grandchildren and make the effort to visit them. I hope to share my life experience without being boring or self-centered - I want my experience to be helpful. I intend to be fun and spunky. I intend to pay attention to all the goodness and not complain about the inevitable aches and pains and deterioration of aging (they're happening already!!). I intend to smile and laugh a lot and play games, like Hearts and Double Solitaire. I do NOT want to be a burden to anyone - I'll be as independent as possible. I intend to keep reading, even with a magnifying glass. I hope to show my gratitude for getting to live as long as I do.... because life is a gift. I believe that if I do these things all along the way, old age might not come as such a shock - rather I'll slide into it with acceptance and some modicum of youthful-like grace!

LESSON 29

EXPECTATIONS FOR NOTE-TAKING, homework ready for discussion.

FINISH DISCUSSION on Lesson 28, points 1-12. Reiterate that we have a choice about how we age, even an obligation to be brave and express our gratitude for the gift of life. Like all the values we wish to teach our children, hope is taught by example. It is possible to be happy as we let go of our younger selves.

DISCUSS HOMEWORK. Who are the old people in your life? Where are they and what are they doing? How much interaction do you have? How do you show your interest in them? What do you admire, or not, about how they handle being old?

Ask for volunteers to read their paragraphs on "When I'm Old." Be prepared to go first. Bear in mind that high school teenagers probably haven't spent a lot of time contemplating mortality, but there's a chance they've had some experience with death so tread carefully. What are they afraid of, if anything?

REMIND THEM of the importance of GOOD HUMOR, MAINTAINING INTEREST IN OTHERS, AND BEING BRAVE AS WE GROW OLD.

COLLECT HOMEWORK.

NOTE

This is an excellent opportunity to arrange for a guest speaker, an old person who is aging with courage, grace, and gratitude. This can be someone you, the teacher, know personally or it can be one of your students' relatives. Explore possibilities. Make it special. Make sure your students are prepared with meaningful, thoughtful questions to ask the guest speaker.

LESSON 30

If you have arranged for a guest speaker, this is the day to do it. ENJOY and make it memorable. Serve tea and bring a special treat. Rearrange the classroom to a more casual, conversational configuration. Have a comfortable chair for your guest.

Whether you have a guest speaker or not, the next activity is a pop quiz.

PASS OUT THE POP QUIZ on chapters 7-12, briefly explain the expectations for answering the questions, answer any of your students' questions, and remind them to use complete sentences, proper spelling, and correct grammar.

PAY ATTENTION. If everyone finishes the quiz and there is class time left, go over the quiz together. Those who finish early can...

READ CHAPTER 13, *TOO SOON OLD, TOO LATE SMART*
                    Happiness is the ultimate risk.

COLLECT THE POP QUIZZES for grading and to be returned tomorrow. Pop quizzes go in the Pocket Folder.

LESSON 30 // POP QUIZ

POP QUIZ #2 ON CHAPTERS 7-12

50 points

Answer the following questions to the best of your ability. Proper grammar and spelling count. Write on the back, if needed.

1. What important skills do we lose when we try to exert control in our intimate relationships?

2. Explain the "paradox of perfection."

3. What is the first step if we want to change ourselves?

4. Explain Freud's theory of the unconscious mind.

5. When should you ask "why?" and when should you ask "why not?"

6. List 3 characteristics of a perfectionist.

7. When it comes to human characteristics, _ _ _ _ _ _ _ _ _ _ is the key.

8. While we like to shift blame for our failures, what is it that we do to protect ourselves from disappointment?

9. What are the 4 steps required for change?

10. Describe the primary task of parents.

LESSON 30 // POP QUIZ cont.

POP QUIZ #2 SAMPLE ANSWER KEY

1. When we exert control in our intimate relationships, we lose the need to negotiate differences; we lose the experience of enduring the uncertainty of failure and rejection; we use power and manipulation to get what we want; we lose touch with the person on the other side of us.

2. In some settings, like work, being a perfectionist is good and helps us be successful and safe (a surgeon or an airplane mechanic), but in our intimate relationships, the paradox is that we gain control only by relinquishing it.

3. The first step to changing ourselves is to understand why we do things, especially undesirable, repetitive behaviors.

4. Freud's theory states that what is going on just below our level of awareness influences our behavior.

5. Ask "why?" when you want to know why you do certain behaviors and ask "why not?" when you are trying to grow and change and have a new experience.

6. Perfectionists keep lists, have perfectionistic attitudes, are more devoted to effort than pleasure, lack flexibility, and are stubborn.

7. m o d e r a t i o n

8. We protect ourselves from disappointment by lowering our expectations.

9. Examine your life; take responsibility for your feelings; decide what you need to do to be happy; do it!!!

10. A primary task of parents throughout their lives is to convey to the young a sense of optimism, to be a role model for hope - to convey that we can be happy amidst the losses and uncertainties of life.

OVERVIEW

LESSONS 31-45

TOO SOON OLD, TOO LATE SMART CHAPTERS

13   Happiness is the ultimate risk.

14   True love is the apple of Eden.

15   Only bad things happen quickly.

16   Not all who wander are lost.

17   Unrequited love is painful but not romantic.

18   There is nothing more pointless, or common, than doing the same things and expecting different results.

HOMEWORK ASSIGNMENTS (3) + samples

- Optimist or Pessimist?
- Who to Pick Letter
- Happiness-producing vs. Bad News Processes

GUEST SPEAKER OPTION

POP QUIZ #3 ON CHAPTERS 13-18

LESSON 31

RETURN GRADED POP QUIZZES. Any questions? Keep in Pocket Folder.

EXPECTATIONS FOR NOTE-TAKING.

READ ALOUD TOGETHER CHAPTER 13, *TOO SOON OLD, TOO LATE SMART*
Happiness is the ultimate risk.

POINTS FOR DISCUSSION

1. Depressed people tend to focus on their "symptoms": sadness, loss of energy, sleep disturbance, appetite changes, diminished capacity for pleasure....and they often resist efforts to improve things. (p. 68)

2. Consider the advantages of being depressed: it is a 'safe' position because your expectations are so low, you are rarely disappointed. (p. 68-69)

3. To be happy is to take the risk of losing that happiness, but all significant accomplishments (invention, exploration, falling in love) require taking risks. We've become a risk-averse society, protected, insulated. (p. 69)

4. It is often hard to sell unhappy people on the idea of taking the chances necessary to alter attitudes and behaviors that play a role in their chronic discouragement. (p. 70)

5. Psychotherapy is "goal-directed conversation in the service of change" and people who come for psychotherapy want change, usually a change in the way they feel (sad, empty, angry, disoriented, anxious, adrift). (p. 70)

6. OUR FEELINGS DEPEND MAINLY ON OUR INTERPRETATION OF WHAT IS HAPPENING TO US AND AROUND US - OUR ATTITUDES. IT IS NOT SO MUCH WHAT OCCURS, BUT HOW WE DEFINE EVENTS AND RESPOND THAT DETERMINES HOW WE FEEL. (p. 70- 71)

7. Those who struggle emotionally have lost, or believe they have lost, their ability to choose those behaviors that will make them happy. (p. 71)

8. Must re-instill HOPE. Ask: what are you looking forward to? (p. 71)

LESSON 31 cont.

9. Without hope, your life shrinks. The truly hopeless contemplate suicide. (p. 71)

10. Dr. Livingston's strategy for dealing with a suicidal person: ask them to examine what it is that has so far kept them from committing suicide, and confront them with the selfishness and anger implied in any act of self-destruction. (p. 71-72)

11. It is an offense to the natural order of life for parents to bury their children. (p. 73)

NOTES:

....

....

....

....

....

....

....

....

....

....

....

....

....

....

....

....

....

LESSON 32

EXPECTATIONS FOR NOTE-TAKING.

REVIEW AND FINISH DISCUSSION from Lesson 31, points 1-11. There is a funny sort of situation in which people often prefer staying stuck in feeling depressed (because it allows them to avoid taking risks) to pulling themselves out of their depression by doing the sometimes-risky things and making the changes that would improve how they feel. Also reinforce that our interpretation and how we respond to events, rather than the events themselves, plays a significant role in how we feel.

DISCUSS HOPELESSNESS. Do you recognize when you are feeling hopeless? What are some signs? What do you do to restore your hope? Think about the people you spend time around - do they tend to be depressed and risk-averse? If so, how does this affect you?

HOMEWORK
Go to Lesson 32 Homework in the Journey Workbook, explain directions.
Due tomorrow, 50 points.

LESSON 32 // HOMEWORK

OPTIMIST OR PESSIMIST?

Due tomorrow, 50 points.

Do you consider yourself to be an optimist or a pessimist? Answer this question by describing a recent event in your life and how you interpreted and responded to it. Typed or neatly handwritten in approximately 250 words.

NOTES:

....

....

....

....

....

....

....

....

....

....

....

....

....

....

....

....

....

....

LESSON 32 // HOMEWORK cont.

OPTIMIST OR PESSIMIST? HOMEWORK SAMPLE

STAYING CENTERED......

One thing that comes with the territory of being divorced is an ex-spouse. If you're lucky, things can go relatively smoothly, the passage of time can dim intense emotions, and people can move on with their lives, hopefully smarter. And the more resolved the two people are about the end of the relationship, the more willing the people are to accept responsibility, the more likely things will go alright. If kids are involved, being resolved and accepting responsibility are magnitudes more important so that, among other things, you can avoid dumping your unresolved garbage and blame on them, so you have a better chance of doing what's best for them.

I've not been lucky in this way, in having a resolved ex-spouse who moved on with his life, and this presented multiple opportunities to either react to the vindictive behavior or to stay centered.

Fortunately, I've been able to stay centered more often than not in the face of incredibly dysfunctional behavior. A key phrase is "more often than not" because I'm human. While most of the time, I stay true to my convictions, my core values, and to the type of person I strive to be, it's not possible to do this 100% of the time. I think there's a good reason for it being this way.

I think there's hope and value both in being centered and in the opportunity presented by falling off-center. I wouldn't know or appreciate one without the other. Also, I wouldn't be presented with the challenge of finding my way back to center, and what I learn about myself and others in doing so, if I never lost my balance. It's an opportunity to cultivate integrity and compassion, and to reinforce core convictions.

I am motivated to be a positive, consistent, loving role model for my kids, and adverse circumstances only serve to strengthen and clarify my determination. When bad, unexpected things happen, which is inevitable, my kids experience me staying calm and centered, and finding center if I temporarily lose my balance. That's hope. That's optimism.

LESSON 33

BRIEFLY DISCUSS homework. Does anyone want to share their story? How many of you feel you are optimists? As we grow older - and hopefully wiser! - it is important to become less reactive and stay dwelling in hope and optimism, in believing that everything will be alright, looking for that opportunity in disguise. On many levels, it's a healthier way to live.

COLLECT HOMEWORK for grading.

EXPECTATIONS FOR NOTE-TAKING.

READ ALOUD TOGETHER CHAPTER 14, *TOO SOON OLD, TOO LATE SMART*
True love is the apple of Eden.

POINTS FOR DISCUSSION

1. Curiosity, weakness, and a desire for each other are traits that make us human. (p. 75)

2. It is amazing that as our innocence (believing in Santa Claus, the Tooth Fairy, and that our parents are perfect) is replaced by a harsher reality (there are Santas in every mall and our parents are not perfect), as we come to see that life is a struggle full of pain and loss with a bad ending (death), we still persist in trying to extract happiness from our brief time on earth. (p. 76)

3. Of all the ways we try to find happiness, "cleaving" to each other brings us closest. (p. 76)

4. DEFINE 'CLEAVE' - to split asunder, to hold fast. It means opposite things!

5. Therapists, who daily deal with the detritus left behind by lost love, can understandably become cynical about the ways people choose those to whom they link their lives. The stories a therapist hears reveal, over and over again, the shallowness and stupidity of our younger selves. (p. 76-77)

6. Where do we learn how to pick a person to link our lives with? There aren't many good examples, and few of us admire what our parents demonstrated in the way of affection and commitment...many doubt the possibility of lasting love. (p. 77)

7. Ironically, when people fall in love, no justification for their attachment is necessary - it

LESSON 33 cont.

is simply accepted that the attraction is beyond explanation and mysterious....so all of us around them accept this and go ahead with the big, expensive celebration. (p. 77)

8. On the other hand, when people fall out of love, an explanation is demanded - what happened? who's at fault? why couldn't you work it out? (p. 77-78)

9. "We didn't love each other anymore" is usually not a sufficient response. (p. 78)

10. To a large extent this is an educational problem. One would think that such an important area of human behavior would be the subject of some consideration in the schools. (p. 78!!)

11. Teach it as a high school course in human personality and behavior that conveys useful information on how to avoid catastrophic mistakes in one's choice of friends and lovers. (p. 78)

12. Trial and error learning when falling in love is costly. (p. 78)

13. Kindness and empathy and how to recognize the presence of these attributes would be discussed. (p. 78)

14. Bromides aside ('we never went to bed angry' or 'moderation in all things'), where is the idea of endless, renewable love? How do we find it and how do we do it? (p. 79)

15. The union of two people offers us the primary compensation for all the burdens of being human: the need to toil, the "thorns and thistles," and the lifelong knowledge of our mortality. (p. 79)

LESSON 34

RETURN GRADED HOMEWORK.

EXPECTATIONS FOR NOTE-TAKING.

REVIEW AND CONTINUE DISCUSSION on Lesson 33, points 1-15. Cultivating in yourself and being able to recognize in others the enduring attributes of kindness and empathy is extremely important. Kindness and empathy are central to growing endless, renewable love.

HOMEWORK

Go to Lesson 34 Homework in the Journey Workbook, explain directions.
Due tomorrow, one page, 50 points.

NOTE

This is another opportunity for a guest speaker. You have some options here: you could pick a person/couple who has been married for 30 or more years or you could pick a person who had a 'successful' divorce or you could pick a person who endured - or is in the middle of - a bitter divorce. Consider your options carefully, choose wisely, and make sure your guest understands what the class is about and is comfortable (in the case of a divorcee) with what you want them to speak about. Also, be sure your students are prepared with thoughtful questions.

LESSON 34 // HOMEWORK

WHO TO PICK LETTER
Due tomorrow, 50 points.

Write a letter to me describing the type of person you are looking to link your life with.
- Why this type?
- Where are you getting your information about who to pick?
- How is this class influencing your thinking about who to pick?

Explain a "before and after" scenario that shows what you are learning.

NOTES:

....

....

....

....

....

....

....

....

....

....

....

....

....

....

....

LESSON 34 // HOMEWORK cont.

WHO TO PICK LETTER HOMEWORK SAMPLE

Dear Ms. Patterson,

First, I want to say that I'm really enjoying this class and the things we're talking about. It's important to know what attributes to look for when picking people, and what to avoid, and I've just never looked very closely at it. One of the big lessons I'm learning is that it takes TIME to get to know someone, for the 'real' person to become apparent. Also, how I feel when I'm with the person is very important. For example, if a guy thinks he's being funny when he puts me down, well, over time I'm really not going to like that because it's not funny, it's mean.

Before this class, I paid more attention to who is cool and popular, thinking that's what I want to be and that's who I want to hang around with. They look like they're having all the fun and getting all this attention. But a lot of those people are jerks. One day they like you and the next day they act like you don't exist. So I'm trying to pay more attention to the people who are pretty consistently nice. They may not be the 'cool crowd,' but they aren't so self-absorbed.

I guess I'm getting most of my information about who to pick from watching my parents and some from listening to my friends, things I read, or movies even though I know that's hollywood. My parents don't communicate much so I don't know if they're good at it or not. I don't see them being affectionate with each other.....and you keep talking about kindness and I don't notice a lot of that either. Mostly they look duty-bound, like they're together because they have been and have to be. I don't see them smiling, touching, or laughing much. It would be helpful to see them having fun together, showing me why they got married in the first place!

So I'm on the lookout for someone who is consistently kind and thoughtful; someone who is flexible and doesn't have to win or be right all the time; someone who is honest and loyal and can look me in the eye when he talks/listens to me; someone who is intelligent and has a variety of interests; someone who enjoys being active and outdoors so we have fun adventures together; someone who doesn't work all the time. What we do when we disagree will be important to pay attention to. I hope we talk and laugh a lot. I hope I feel safe to be my true self when we're together, and that we grow closer as we change and grow old.

Sincerely,
Your Student

LESSON 35

COLLECT HOMEWORK. Write a thoughtful response to each of their letters.

If you have arranged for a guest speaker, this is the day to do it. Like last time, prepare your classroom, set an inviting tone, make your guest comfortable, serve tea and a special treat like muffins, and jump right into the conversation. Be prepared to steer it and keep things moving. If you do not have a guest speaker lined up, proceed with the following lesson.

EXPECTATIONS FOR NOTE-TAKING.

READ ALOUD TOGETHER CHAPTER 15, *TOO SOON OLD, TOO LATE SMART*
                    Only bad things happen quickly.

POINTS FOR DISCUSSION

1. It is a common fantasy that change in our lives can be achieved quickly. Once we "know" what to do, we ought to just be able to do it.....but sudden transformations are rare. (p. 80)

2. The most familiar behaviors that resist change are addictions like drinking, smoking, and drugs (chemical addictions), but also gambling, overeating, shopping, and sex - not chemical, but addictions all the same. (p. 80-81)

3. The psychological power of habit, particularly bad habits, insinuates itself over time and makes it extremely difficult to change, even when the habit threatens to destroy our lives. (p. 81)

4. Among our maladaptive behaviors are our habitual ways of relating to others
    - THE TRAITS THAT WE DISPLAY TOWARD OTHER PEOPLE ARE MAJOR DETERMINANTS OF HOW SUCCESSFUL WE ARE IN FORMING AND SUSTAINING RELATIONSHIPS. (p. 81)

5. Most of our personal style is not the product of conscious choice - these elements are either inborn or were formed by our early experience with our families. Because they exist below the level of our conscious minds, they are resistant to change, even when they aren't working for us. (p. 81-82)

6. ANY PROCESS DIRECTED AT CHANGING, EVEN A LITTLE, OUR WELL-ESTABLISHED PATTERNS OF THINKING AND BEHAVING IS GOING TO TAKE

LESSON 35 cont.

TIME BECAUSE IT INVOLVES EFFORTS AT GAINING INSIGHT, REEVALUATING BEHAVIORS, TRYING NEW APPROACHES, AND TRANSLATING NEW KNOWLEDGE INTO NEW BEHAVIORS. (p. 82)

7. The things that alter our lives in a moment are seldom good news. Virtually all the happiness-producing processes in our lives take time, usually a long time: learning new things, changing old behaviors, building satisfying relationships, raising children. This is why PATIENCE AND DETERMINATION are among life's primary virtues. (p. 82-83)

8. Instant gratification - we're led to believe we can buy happiness and the good life through the right car, the right house and lots of botox...so most of us are in debt, still not beautiful like the magazines, still not happy, and still going to die one day. (p. 83)

9. Somewhere along the line we became an impatient people, but there are rarely quick answers to all difficulties. (p. 83-84)

10. We have to come to terms with the losses that life inevitably imposes upon us. Primary among these is the loss of our younger selves. Many of us go for youth and devalue the knowledge and perspective that should come with our accumulated life experience. (p. 84-85)

11. We have short attention spans, our memories are limited, and we focus on the foreground. We pay attention to a limited number of young, good-looking, and wealthy people who fill the pages of our magazines...what about the rest of us? (p. 85)

12. As long as we measure ourselves by what we have and how we look, life is an inevitably discouraging experience, characterized by greed, envy, and a desire to be someone else. (p. 85)

13. Our actions define us, not our causes; consider the 'causes' that justify killing.

14. THE TENSION BETWEEN WANTING THINGS TO BE SIMPLE AND OUR WILLINGNESS TO EXPEND EFFORT TO CHANGE WORKS ITSELF OUT IN OUR

LESSON 35 cont.

DAILY LIVES....AND BECAUSE THE PROCESS OF BUILDING HAS ALWAYS BEEN SLOWER AND MORE COMPLICATED THAN THAT OF DESTRUCTION, IF WE BELIEVE IN SUDDEN TRANSFORMATION OR THE BIG SCORE, WE ARE LESS LIKELY TO PURSUE THE HARDER AND LESS IMMEDIATELY SATISFYING WORK OF BECOMING THE PEOPLE WE WANT TO BE. (p. 86)

TIME + PATIENCE + REFLECTION =
A SATISFYING WAY THROUGH LIFE

NOTES:

....

....

....

....

....

....

....

....

....

....

....

....

....

....

....

....

LESSON 36

RETURN THEIR GRADED LETTERS. Have them share a few things they are learning about who to pick.

EXPECTATIONS FOR NOTE-TAKING.

REVIEW AND FINISH DISCUSSION on Lesson 35, points 1-14. There are many very important points in this chapter so allow time for thorough note-taking and questions. Reinforce that just as it takes time for behavior patterns to become apparent when getting to know someone, it also takes time to change our own deeply-ingrained habits - there's no quick fix. Much of what we do and who we are is either inborn or was formed by our early experience with our families so it exists below the surface, below our conscious mind, we're often not even aware of what we're doing! Even with consciousness, it takes patience and determination to change who we are. And if it's something we can't change, we can at least manage the behavior more mindfully.

INTRODUCE the homework assignment, reiterating the points about happiness-producing processes taking a long time because of what is involved, and that usually only bad things happen quickly. Ask for examples, personal or not, that illustrate these points (winning the lottery is an exception!).

HOMEWORK
Go to Lesson 36 Homework in the Journey Workbook, explain directions.
Due in one week, one page minimum, 100 points.

LESSON 36 // HOMEWORK

HAPPINESS-PRODUCING VS. BAD NEWS PROCESSES

Due in one week, one page minimum, 100 points.

Drawing on your life experience, write about a happiness-producing process and a bad news experience. It's not so much the experiences themselves that I'm interested in, but rather how the experiences affected you, your emotional reaction, the character traits that emerged, and what you learned about yourself.

What did the experience set in motion? Write about what worked and what wasn't effective....or if you're still in the process, write about how it's going, where you might be getting hung up, what motivates you to keep going. Compare and contrast the two experiences. Get under the surface here, take a look at what really went on or is going on.

Remember: Learning from our experiences so we come closer to getting it right the next time is the only consolation for the pain and struggle of life's challenges.

LESSON 36 // HOMEWORK cont.

HAPPINESS-PRODUCING VS. BAD NEWS PROCESSES HOMEWORK SAMPLE

One of the best happiness-producing processes that I am engaged in is raising my two sons. They are 15 and 13 now and it has been a wonderfully rewarding and challenging experience - tiring, too, because it requires so much energy and patience all of the time. Much of parenting is tedious and repetitious, particularly when they're babies, but patience is necessary to grow a healthy, safe feeling, a trust in the world. As they get older, it requires patience to answer their endless questions and help them make sense of the world and how it works. 'Yes' or 'no' is incomplete and an irritated tone of voice sends a counter-productive message - they need explanations, sometimes when I'm least in the mood to offer them. Then, as they begin connecting their thinking with emotion, patience is again important when supporting them through emotional experiences so they learn about feelings, how to express them, how others express them, and how our behavior affects other people.

Now, all these years later, parenting still requires patience, but it comes easily because my sons are such interesting, curious, respectful, and fun people. Because I consistently gave them my time and attention from the beginning, they feel safe and secure, they feel loved, they're open to and optimistic about life. They have learned patience, and almost daily, I catch glimpses that patience pays huge dividends. They're fun to be around, they show appreciation, and discipline is hardly an issue. We respect each other. I am grateful that we are at ease and have so much fun together.

A significant bad news process I went through happened when the guy I was dating broke off our relationship. It caught me off-guard and for awhile I couldn't stop crying. I felt lost, lonely, impossibly sad, I couldn't sleep well, food was tasteless and uninteresting. Eventually I was able to think more clearly. While it was messy on one level, on a deeper level, I believed, based on how we were getting to know each other, that we came together for positive reasons, and that we could tame old patterns when they showed up.

So I chose not to write him off. I chose to be his friend, to be patient.....so often we're in such a hurry that we don't give ourselves and others time to figure things out, to think about what really matters and how we really feel, to see what we're capable of. It was

LESSON 36 // HOMEWORK cont.

a leap of faith, something I'd never done before. It was tempting to just write him off and eventually find someone else (how original!!), but I was curious and I wasn't in a hurry. It ended up being only a few months of my life that things were uncertain, and in that time and space, we figured out our hearts and what mattered.

Patience and staying open are interesting mind states. It's so easy to just react, give up, and shut down - which leads to a bunch of predictable stuff. Openness brings possibility and the unknown. Patience allows time for things to unfold, for people to find their way.

LESSON 37

Any questions about yesterday's homework assignment? Encourage your students to ask for help. It's good practice!!

EXPECTATIONS FOR NOTE-TAKING.

READ ALOUD TOGETHER CHAPTER 16, *TOO SOON OLD, TOO LATE SMART*
Not all who wander are lost.

POINTS FOR DISCUSSION

1. We are a linear, goal-oriented people - we like the straightest path to our goals. (p. 87)

2. Our education system creates the linear structure and the rules: obey authority (teachers), work hard, and cooperate with others. We are "taught to do what we are told until sufficient time elapses that we are allowed to tell others what to do." (p. 87)

3. OF ALL THE THINGS THAT DEFINE US, EDUCATION SEEMS TO BE THE MOST HIGHLY CORRELATED WITH SUCCESS - no wonder we're told to do well in school, follow instructions, please others, and obey the rules. Implicit in this process is the promise that doing these things will bring happiness. (p. 88)

4. Very often, after buying into this system for 20, 30 or 40 years, we feel that the promise wasn't kept, we're not happy, the things we aspired to now feel like a burden, and we become preoccupied with what we missed along the way. (p. 88)

5. Frequently, sex is one of the things that got neglected in a linear, goal-directed life. Men, whose sense of themselves is closely tied to feelings of sexual adequacy, long for excitement, which in part explains the 'mid-life crisis' of affairs and sports cars. (p. 88)

6. The rebellious 60s and 70s were a time of dropping out, casual sex, anti-war protests, shunning materialism, and not pursuing the traditional paths to success. Turns out, many of these rebellious young people grew up to be white-collar professionals like their parents! (p. 89)

7. Still today there is a core of adventurous people willing to step off the traditional

LESSON 37 cont.

educational path, to see the world, to educate themselves in ways not possible in the classroom. (homeschool, Peace Corps, join the military, etc.) (p. 89)

8. Later in life, career changes, marital misadventures, or spiritual explorations can seem like forms of "wandering" because they depart from the norm, but they may also be an EXPRESSION OF COURAGE TO TAKE RISKS IN THE STRUGGLE TO FIND THE HAPPINESS AND MEANING THAT DIDN'T HAPPEN ALONG THE TRADITIONAL JOURNEY. (p. 89)

9. Being compassionate, nonjudgmental, and patient is important. We all struggle, we're all trying to get it right and "find ourselves," and life doesn't follow a straight and narrow line. There is learning in the curves.

10. OFTEN IT IS THE DALLIANCES AND THE DETOURS THAT DEFINE US. THERE ARE NO MAPS TO GUIDE OUR MOST IMPORTANT SEARCHES; WE MUST RELY ON HOPE, CHANCE, INTUITION, AND A WILLINGNESS TO BE SURPRISED. (p. 90)

REMINDER: Keep working on your "happiness-producing and bad news processes" essay.

LESSON 38

EXPECTATIONS FOR NOTE-TAKING.

REVIEW AND FINISH DISCUSSION on Lesson 37, points 1-10. While our education system is linear and gives us clear marching orders (show up, follow directions, work hard, please others, obey the rules, etc.) that, if followed, will supposedly lead to happiness, life isn't always linear. Often our most important learning occurs when we detour from the linear path.

If you have some extra time, have them organize their Journey Workbooks and Pocket Folders, see if anything is missing......there will be another check soon.

REMINDER: Keep working on your essay.

NOTES:

....

....

....

....

....

....

....

....

....

....

....

....

....

LESSON 39

REMINDER: How's it going with the "happiness-producing process vs. bad news experience" essay? It is due the day after tomorrow.

EXPECTATIONS FOR NOTE-TAKING.

READ ALOUD TOGETHER CHAPTER 17, *TOO SOON OLD, TOO LATE SMART*
Unrequited love is painful but not romantic.

POINTS FOR DISCUSSION

1. First, DEFINE 'UNREQUITED' - not returned or reciprocated.

2. We have all had experience with/felt the sting of unrequited love, or the longing for what we cannot have.

3. Childhood and adolescent crushes that are not reciprocated give way to adult searches for the perfect partner, someone to complete us, to affirm our worth, and whose love will warm us in our old age. (p. 91)

4. It starts with seeking the unconditional approval of the good parent, the ultimate emotional security. If we got this as a child, we want it again; if, like most of us, we didn't, we still wish for it as a shield in an uncertain, often uncaring world. Sometimes we project our need for love onto another and ignore the fact that it is not being returned! (p. 92)

5. We often project this need for love in very unusual and unproductive places, sadly, even on people we don't know, which is romantic/fantasy love blurring into obsession. (p. 92)

6. THE KEY DIFFERENCE BETWEEN ROMANTIC LOVE AND OBSESSION IS THAT AN OBSESSION CAN RESIDE IN ONE PERSON ALONE. (p. 92)

7. Battered women and those for whom a dead relationship is still the subject of endless contemplation/conversation show a love that will not die. On first glance this may sound admirable, on second glance, not. It's as if proclaiming undying devotion

LESSON 39 cont.

dignifies what could otherwise be taken for an unattractive masochism! It's definitely not romantic. (p. 93)

8. THE MYTH OF "LOVE AT FIRST SIGHT" SETS US UP FOR DISAPPOINTMENT - THAT SUDDEN, DIZZYING WAVE OF FEELING CAN SHORT-CIRCUIT THE TASK OF BUILDING A FRIENDSHIP THAT CAN DEEPEN INTO SOMETHING EVEN MORE ELECTRIFYING. "LOVE AT FIRST SIGHT" TAKES HARDLY ANY TIME. (p. 93)

9. The task of building a friendship takes time, attentiveness, and some level of rational thought....a less easy to comprehend emotion can be there too, but this doesn't mean we're stepping off a cliff in the dark. It's possible to fall and understand a bit about the falling! (p. 93)

10. WHAT GIVES LOVE ITS POWER IS THAT IT IS SHARED. When experienced alone, it may be intense, as is any form of loneliness, but it is not likely to last or result in any useful behavior, and is of limited interest to others. Again, nothing about it is romantic. (p. 93)

REMINDER: The essay........due soon.

NOTES:

....

....

....

....

....

....

....

....

....

LESSON 40

EXPECTATIONS FOR NOTE-TAKING.

REVIEW AND FINISH DISCUSSION on Lesson 39, points 1-10. Unrequited love, love that is not returned, is a dead end, a fantasy. What makes it romantic love is that it is shared and it takes time to grow. Pay attention to "love at first sight" - enjoy the dizzying feeling but root it in something real by getting to know the person. Does the dizzying feeling turn into something deeper or does it just fizzle and you lose interest?

TALK ABOUT UNREQUITED LOVE and their experiences with it. Have you ever had a crush on someone? What did that look like? How did you recognize it was time to move on? Were friends rolling their eyes and telling you to get over it? Did something hurtful/ embarrassing happen? Discuss some of the unhealthy behavior and thought patterns we do when we're swimming in unrequited love - denying reality, how we "lie" to ourselves, etc. - and how we can move out of that unhealthy, one-sided, lonely place.

REMINDER: Your essay on a happiness-producing process and a bad news experience is due tomorrow.

NOTES:

....

....

....

....

....

....

....

....

....

....

....

....

LESSON 41

COLLECT HOMEWORK ESSAYS.

EXPECTATIONS FOR NOTE-TAKING.

READ ALOUD TOGETHER CHAPTER 18, *TOO SOON OLD, TOO LATE SMART*

There is nothing more pointless, or common, than doing
the same things and expecting different results.

POINTS FOR DISCUSSION

1. Mistakes are a consequence of being human and are an important element of trial and error learning. Some errors have more serious consequences, but few are hopeless and irredeemable. (p. 95)

2. It is frustrating to make the same mistake over and over again, something we often do when picking a person to be intimate with. For example, one would think we would be smarter in picking a spouse the second time around, but the divorce rate of subsequent marriages exceeds the 50% of first marriages! (p. 95-96)

3. What is behind these numbers? We may be 20 years older, we've finished school, we've had a career - in some respects we've learned a lot. But we haven't gained equivalent insight into who we are and why we choose the people we do. Think about it: we make a choice, we stick with it, and most of us don't spend much time reflecting on why we made the choice. The opportunity to practice and gain insight into who we choose is before we say "I do." After we say "I do," the trick is to stay mindful of why we chose the person we did and grow through life's changes and uncertainties. (p. 96)

4. AN IMPORTANT COMPONENT IN ANY LEARNING PROCESS IS NOT SO MUCH ACCUMULATING ANSWERS, BUT FIGURING OUT THE RIGHT QUESTIONS TO ASK. (p. 96)

5. Psychotherapy takes on a Q & A format on purpose - it is a joint exploration in understanding motives and patterns of thought and behavior, of trying to make connections between past influences and present conceptions of what it is we want and how best to get it. (p. 96)

LESSON 41 cont.

6.   Remember, most human behavior is driven by intentions that are below the level of our awareness; for example, we 'forget' our dentist appointment. (p. 96)

7.   NEARLY EVERY HUMAN ACTION IS IN SOME WAY AN EXPRESSION OF HOW WE THINK ABOUT OURSELVES. Few behaviors are self-esteem neutral. Strive to bring more awareness to your intentions. (p. 97)

8.   When facing an important life decision, learn to ask yourself: "How will this make me feel about myself?" In a relationship ask: "How does being with this person make me feel?" (p. 97)

9.   Our repetitive mistakes are most noticeable in the family dramas that play out over and over again in a way that suggests long rehearsal. They can almost always be traced back to a direction, criticism or outright insult that the other person reacted to with predictable antagonism. We feel a need to defend ourselves. (p. 97-98)

10.   So, over time, our closest relationships resemble power struggles. Gone is the sense of shared fate. Instead we battle to maintain our self-respect, which is being threatened by the person who knows us best. Who would want to live this way? (p. 98)

11.   Yet when people are asked to stop the disparaging remarks, they shift responsibility for change from themselves to "the other." Everyone wants peace but no one wants to go first. (p. 98-99)

12.   If asked what you lose by trying, we often wonder how long we have to try instead of asking "why would I live with someone I don't trust?" The answer to the latter question brings up all the reasons we coexist unhappily for years - money, concerns for children, fear of being alone, simple inertia - so we avoid asking it. (p. 99)

13.   Mistrust is at the heart of such relationships and the only way out is to try something different....but we have such a low expectation of happiness that we avoid taking

LESSON 41 cont.

emotional risks. Why take an emotional risk if we think the goal - happiness - is impossible? (p. 99)

14. The exercise of change goes better when it is shared.

15. Even if we're cynical about improvement in our own lives, most of us wish for something better for our children. If so, and given that children learn most of what they know about life from observing their parents, we must try to set examples of kindness, tolerance, and conflict resolution. (p. 99-100)

16. Here is where the concept of repetitive behaviors comes in: if what you have done in the past produces unsatisfying outcomes, why not try a new approach? The new approach isn't the same, theoretical, standard thing for every relationship - it depends on what works for the people in the relationship. Be practical: If what you are doing now isn't working, why not try something else? Your kids are watching you! Be open. (p. 100)

NOTES:

....

....

....

....

....

....

....

....

....

....

LESSON 42

EXPECTATIONS FOR NOTE-TAKING.

REVIEW AND FINISH DISCUSSION on Lesson 41, points 1-16. Once again, there are a LOT of important points to get down so be sure your students take good notes (pop quiz material!). The frustration (not to mention the eventual disconnect from ourselves and others) we experience in repeating the same mistake over and over again should be a wake-up call to take a closer look at what's driving the repetitive behaviors. After a long power struggle, and with mistrust and low expectations for achieving happiness keeping us stuck, we are reminded of the two questions 'why?' and 'why not?' - the one to ask when contemplating change is 'why not?' If what you are doing now isn't working, why not try something different? Who wants to live with someone they don't trust? What can you do differently to move more into trust?

RETURN GRADED HOMEWORK and discuss. Ask for volunteers to share either a happiness-producing process or a bad news experience.

DROP A HINT.........there might be a pop quiz coming....

LESSONS 43 & 44

ROLE PLAYING EXERCISE: TALK ABOUT family dramas. What is a recurring "theme song" in your family dynamics? Brainstorm examples such as 'you're not good enough' or 'you need a lot of advice' or 'why can't you be more like _ _ _ _ _?' or 'you just don't care about me,' etc. Run through a sample role play.

Split the class into groups of 2 or 3, give them some time to plan and practice, and then ROLE PLAY THE DRAMAS.

After each role play, 1) have the students trace back to the trigger - the direction, criticism or insult that started the drama - and 2) offer suggestions for moving to a healthier pattern that will hopefully, eventually stop or diffuse the repetitive drama. It is important to pay attention to both sides of the drama to get at what's driving it, i.e. both the person who made the trigger remark and the other person's response.

QUESTIONS TO GUIDE THE PROCESS

1. What is the emotional state of the person who made the offensive comment (tired? sick? PMS? stress at work? etc.) What is the history behind it?
2. Did the person on defense throw more gas on the fire with their response? WAYS WE ESCALATE A DRAMA: tone of voice; blame; return the insult; disrespectful attitude; stop listening; body language/facial expressions; silence/leave the room; shut down; exaggerate the issue; attach another issue; sarcasm; threaten and act superior; say "If I were you.....''; public assassination/embarrassment; ask "why did you do that?"
3. How can you break the cycle of blame, of feeling you need to protect yourself from the other person? What is a loving thing to say or do? Will a hug work? We all have repetitive thought and behavior patterns and we all struggle with them. WAYS TO DIFFUSE THE DRAMA: cultivate compassion, not blame (what is upsetting this person that makes them act this way?); accept responsibility, apologize if needed; take a breath, create a pause; practice becoming less reactive; practice listening; finish the conversation; be a win-win person. At the end, is there space for some humor?

Take two class periods to complete this activity. Be thorough.

LESSON 45

PASS OUT THE POP QUIZ on chapters 13-18, briefly explain the expectations for answering the questions, answer any of your students' questions, and remind them to use complete sentences, proper spelling, and correct grammar.

PAY ATTENTION If everyone finishes the quiz and there is class time left, go over the quiz together. Those who finish early can...

READ CHAPTER 19, *TOO SOON OLD, TOO LATE SMART*
We flee from the truth in vain.

COLLECT THE POP QUIZZES for grading and to be returned tomorrow. Graded pop quizzes go in the Pocket Folder.

NOTES:

....

....

....

....

....

....

....

....

....

....

....

....

....

LESSON 45 // POP QUIZ

POP QUIZ #3 ON CHAPTERS 13-18

50 points

Answer the following questions to the best of your ability. Proper grammar and spelling count. Write on the back, if needed.

1. What is a primary driver of our feelings and whether or not we struggle emotionally?

2. What is the greatest risk of being happy?

3. What is the irony of falling in and out of love?

4. What four steps are involved in changing well-established patterns of thinking and behavior?

5. Two of life's primary virtues are _ _ _ _ _ _ _ and _ _ _ _ _ _ _ _ _ _ _ _.

6. What is the problem with being impatient?

7. What is a drawback of a linear, goal-directed path?

8. What gives love its power?

9. Why does psychotherapy take on a Q and A format?

10. List four reasons why people coexist unhappily in relationships - what holds people in place?

LESSON 45 // POP QUIZ cont.

POP QUIZ #3 SAMPLE ANSWER KEY

1. Our feelings depend mainly on our interpretation of what is happening to us and around us. How we define events and respond determines how we feel.

2. The greatest risk of being happy is losing the happiness...which hurts.

3. When we fall in love, we rarely have to explain or justify it, but when we fall out of love, an explanation is demanded. "We fell out of love" isn't enough.

4. First, work at gaining insight, look at what you do. Second, re-evaluate behaviors - what is working and what isn't? Third, try new approaches - does this work better? Fourth, translate new knowledge to new behaviors = CHANGE.

5. p a t i e n c e and d e t e r m i n a t i o n

6. The problem with being impatient is that we want a quick and easy fix to our problems, we want to buy happiness, but it just doesn't work that way. Time, patience, and reflection are necessary for a satisfying way through life. Good things take time.

7. The drawback to a linear, goal-directed path is that sooner or later we start to wonder what we missed, what we could have learned by taking a detour. Detours don't necessarily mean dropping out of life - they're another way to learn.

8. Love gets its power in being shared with another person.

9. A Q and A format sets up a joint exploration for making connections between past influences and present conceptions. Asking questions helps us understand what motivates us and what is influencing our thoughts and behavior.

10. Money; concerns for children; fear of being alone; simple inertia.

OVERVIEW

LESSONS 46-57

TOO SOON OLD, TOO LATE SMART CHAPTERS

19 We flee from the truth in vain.

20 It's a poor idea to lie to oneself.

21 We are all prone to the myth of the perfect stranger.

22 Love is never lost, not even in death.

23 Nobody likes to be told what to do.

24 The major advantage of illness is that it provides relief from responsibility.

HOMEWORK ASSIGNMENTS (3) + samples
- Cognitive Dissonance
- Journey Workbook/Pocket Folder Check #2
- Letter about Criticism or Gratitude

POP QUIZ #4 ON CHAPTERS 19-24

LESSON 46

RETURN GRADED POP QUIZZES. Any questions? Keep in Pocket Folder.
Take a break from note-taking.

READ ALOUD TOGETHER CHAPTER 19, *TOO SOON OLD, TOO LATE SMART*
We flee from the truth in vain.

In this chapter, Dr. Livingston talks about his experience with learning he was adopted. No one told him, the truth was kept a secret. Use his experience to illustrate the effects of withholding the truth, and his conviction that "knowing was better than not knowing."

- What sorts of things do we keep secret?
- Why do we keep secrets? Why don't we just say? (role of fear)
- Talk about short-term vs. long-term consequences of a secret.
- What does it feel like to keep a secret?
- What is the first question we invariably ask when the secret is finally revealed? (Why didn't you tell me?)
- What are the benefits of knowing the truth?
- Does the truth have a way of making itself known eventually?

Cultivate compassion here - remind them how difficult it is to suspend judgment, to truly put yourself in someone else's experience, and try to understand the emotions driving a difficult decision.

Sometimes we make mistakes.....how forgiving and compassionate can you be? Remember, you get what you give....and it seems to all come around in a big karmic circle.

"If only I could speak with him for a moment, to tell him that things turned out all right, that something good came from his passionate mistake." (p. 106)

LESSON 47

EXPECTATIONS FOR NOTE-TAKING.

READ ALOUD TOGETHER CHAPTER 20, *TOO SOON OLD, TOO LATE SMART*

It's a poor idea to lie to oneself.

POINTS FOR DISCUSSION

1. DEFINE 'AUTHENTICITY.' Real. When your actions are in accord with your words.

2. We like to see ourselves as having a relatively stable identity that expresses our core values over time. The opinion of people we respect and who matter most to us is very important. (p. 107)

3. DEFINE 'HYPOCRISY.' A pretense of having some desirable or publicly-approved attitude; a pretense of having a virtuous character that one does not really possess.

4. Few human attributes excite more contempt than hypocrisy. People whose actions don't line up with their words become the objects of derision. Cite examples of the disconnect between words and behavior: adulterous preachers, deceitful politicians, drug-abusing moralists, pedophile priests. (p. 107-108)

5. WORSE THAN THE CONCEALMENT OF EMBARRASSING MORAL LAPSES ARE THE INTERPRETATIONS THAT ALLOW US TO CONTINUE DOING THINGS THAT ERODE OUR SENSE OF OURSELVES. In other words, the stories or lies we tell ourselves to avoid looking closely at our behaviors, i.e. "it was an accident," or "what a coincidence," or "I forgot." (p. 108)

6. DENIAL is another way people lie to themselves. Look at people indulging in addictions - they often say they don't have a problem and can quit anytime, assertions that fly in the face of a catastrophic decline in their lives: DWIs, broken marriages, lost jobs. (p. 108)

7. It is understandable to feel a need to lie to others about our behaviors, but lying to ourselves completely disables us from making needed changes. (p. 108)

8. DEFINE 'INTENTION.' Purpose or attitude. The mental action connected to a behavior.

LESSON 47 cont.

9. New Year's resolutions and other promises we make to ourselves are some of the most damaging lies because they are distractions from the serious task of evaluating who we are and what we really want. (p. 109)

10. Luck and excuses: While chance certainly plays a role in life, IT IS AN ACT OF LAZINESS TO SAY THAT MOST OF WHAT HAPPENS TO US IS LUCK. People are reluctant to take responsibility for themselves, PREFERRING EXCUSES TO DIFFICULT SELF-EXAMINATION. (p. 109)

11. Talk about 'death by stupidity' - driving drunk, diseases related to smoking or obesity, accidental discharge of firearms. (p. 110)

12. The truth may not make us free, but TO LIE TO OURSELVES IN THE NAME OF TEMPORARY COMFORT IS THE ULTIMATE FOLLY. While this may seem like a benign form of dishonesty because no one else is cheated or disadvantaged, LIFE DECISIONS THAT ARE NOT BASED ON REALITY ARE BOUND TO BE FAULTY AND CREATE UNHAPPINESS. (p. 110)

13. It is difficult, if not impossible, to see ourselves plainly - it's tough to escape a rationalization or two. (p. 110)

14. IT IS WHEN THE DREAM OF WHAT WE COULD BE COLLIDES WITH THE TRUTH OF WHAT WE ARE THAT THE CLANG OF COGNITIVE DISSONANCE BOTH DEAFENS AND BLINDS US. (p. 110)

LESSON 48

EXPECTATIONS FOR NOTE-TAKING.

REVIEW AND FINISH DISCUSSION on Lesson 47, points 1-14. Go over the different ways we lie to ourselves and how this affects our behavior and ultimately our happiness.

DISCUSS COGNITIVE DISSONANCE What does it mean? What does it feel like? What does it look like? Talk about the symptoms of being out of alignment, not authentic: tone of voice, eye contact, stress level, ease, patience, consistency, reliability, etc.

HOMEWORK

Go to Lesson 48 Homework in the Journey Workbook, explain directions.
Due tomorrow, 50 points.

NOTES:

....

....

....

....

....

....

....

....

....

....

....

....

....

....

LESSON 48 // HOMEWORK

COGNITIVE DISSONANCE

Due tomorrow, 50 points.

In 250 words or less, write about the cognitive dissonance going on in your life. First, take an honest look. What stories or lies do you tell yourself?

For example:

- What are your typical New Year's resolutions or goals and how have they gone?
- Do you follow through?
- When you don't, what do you tell yourself?
- Another way to look at it is what are you avoiding?
- Is there a conversation you need to have with someone, a relationship that needs attention, something you need to do? If so, what are you telling yourself in order to continue avoiding it?

Second, take the next step and write about how you will deal with the cognitive dissonance - what do you want to do and how will you do it? The more conscious we are of our intentions and the person we strive to be, the more likely we are to behave in accordance with our intentions.....thereby quieting the cognitive dissonance and becoming more authentic.

LESSON 48 // HOMEWORK cont.

COGNITIVE DISSONANCE HOMEWORK SAMPLE

For the most part, there's not much cognitive dissonance in my brain and life right now. I have a lot of clarity about my life, how I got here, and the kind of person I strive to be so my behavior is pretty consistently aligned with my thoughts, words, and feelings. Some days I flow better than others, and noticing that keeps me awake and paying attention. It's a huge relief to feel so calm, centered, and better able to enjoy my life.

But there was a time when there was plenty of chaos. I was telling myself I was happy and had a great life - nice house, "successful" husband, cool vacations, etc. It looked great on the surface, but underneath I was incredibly sad and unsettled. I kept telling myself I was happy - or would be when this or that finally happened or when this ended or whatever - but that story just wasn't panning out. I did love being a mom, and adored and had fun with my kids, but if I saw a movie of myself then, it would be painful and I wouldn't recognize myself.

A lot of "stories" I was telling myself were holding me in place, and denial and avoidance played a part. I kept thinking something was wrong with me (postpartum depression, lack of sleep, etc.) - and I worried about disapproval, there was pressure to "make the best of it." The biggest story I was telling myself was that it was the "responsible" thing to stay put, shut up, and do my job. How important is happiness anyway? Better to be RESPONSIBLE, especially with kids involved. But it started to feel really wrong. How could I possibly teach my sons about love, trust, ease, kindness, joy, etc. if I wasn't experiencing them myself?! The unhappiness could no longer be avoided.

I took myself to task and got help. I looked at what I was doing and where/how I learned it. I changed some things, big and small, that weren't working. I got divorced. I'm more authentic now in that my emotions and behavior are integrated. I am a positive example of all those emotions that weren't being experienced or expressed before. Really, I just make more sense to myself and others. Understanding makes it so much easier to be happy.

LESSON 49

COLLECT HOMEWORK.

EXPECTATIONS FOR NOTE-TAKING.

READ ALOUD TOGETHER CHAPTER 21, *TOO SOON OLD, TOO LATE SMART*

We are all prone to the myth of the perfect stranger.

POINTS FOR DISCUSSION

1. Nothing causes more dissatisfaction in our lives than thinking that, in our youth, we made the wrong choice of a partner. (p. 111)

2. In our dissatisfaction, we generate a lot of fantasies about there being a person out there who will save us with his or her love, and much of the infidelity in unhappy marriages rests on this illusion. (p. 111)

3. Such high estimates of infidelity by age 40 (50-65% of men and 35-45% of women) reflect both a high level of hypocrisy in a society whose dominant expressed marital value is monogamy and a high level of dissatisfaction with our partners. (p. 111-112)

4. What are people looking for outside their marriages? Apart from variety, we're looking for reassurance, for experiences that feed our conceit that we are still attractive. Feeling attractive and having sex with someone new is a way to push back against aging and mortality. (p. 112)

5. HEALTHY MATURATION ALLOWS US TO INTERNALIZE A BELIEF THAT WE ARE UNIQUELY VALUABLE AND GIVES US A STABLE SENSE OF A LOVABLE SELF. (p. 112)

6. We want unconditional love and we seldom get it; it is a source of discontent in most marriages. (p. 112)

7. What passes for love between most adults more often resembles a kind of unspoken contract for services: the man provides financial security and the woman provides housekeeping, sex, and childcare. (p. 112-113)

LESSON 49 cont.

8. The women's movement accomplished some important things, but it seems to have created a heightened sense of resentment and competition. A woman's desire to 'seize' power is not a prescription for closeness. (p. 113)

9. Financial independence means more people are less likely to be trapped in unsatisfying relationships, and any social development that increases our choices seems like an improvement....but there is a sense that we have lost something. (p. 113)

10. First, there is the damage that is being inflicted on children. Divorce can cause insecurity and unhappiness for children, particularly since most of the time there is some level of bitterness and recrimination between the parents. Kids can cope with their lives being turned upside down, but that doesn't change the devastation and disillusionment that most of them experience. (p. 113-114)

11. Because of the potential damage to children and financial considerations, most infidelity is not done in anticipation of divorce though that is often the result. (p. 114)

12. While nearly all animal species engage in a kind of promiscuity, infidelity is a uniquely human expression of fear and longing. The search for ideal love is both infantile and a symptom of middle-aged fears. Most often, infidelity fails to improve our lives and very often devastates them, but that does not dissuade us from trying. (p. 114)

LESSON 50

RETURN GRADED HOMEWORK ESSAYS on cognitive dissonance. Ask for a couple volunteers to share their essays...or just talk about cognitive dissonance some more.

EXPECTATIONS FOR NOTE-TAKING.

FINISH DISCUSSION on Lesson 49, points 1-12. We rarely find what we want - at least on a lasting basis - when we look outside our marriage, but that doesn't stop a lot of people from looking. It is often devastating for the children involved.

If there's time, **GO TO** JOURNEY CHECKLIST #2 in the Journey Workbook. Briefly go over what is expected for this, and their **HOMEWORK** tonight is to organize their workbooks and folders for the check tomorrow, 50 points.

NOTES:

....

....

....

....

....

....

....

....

....

....

....

....

....

LESSON 50 // JOURNEY CHECKLIST #2

- **JW/PF CHECK #1**

- **LESSONS 15 & 16** Notes, flow chart, and Reflections on Chapter 6

- **POP QUIZ #1** (Pocket Folder)

- **LESSON 18** Reflections on Chapter 7

- **LESSONS 19 & 20** Notes and Reflections on Chapter 8

- **LESSONS 21 & 22** Notes and Reflections on Chapter 9

- **LESSONS 23 & 24** Notes and Reflections on Chapter 10

- **COMPLETED EMOTIONAL MENU PROJECT** and grade sheet (Pocket Folder)

- **LESSON 24** Homework - Personal Ad

- **LESSONS 26 & 27** Notes and Reflections on Chapter 11

- **LESSON 26** Homework - notes on self-imposed constraints

- **LESSONS 28 & 29** Notes and Reflections on Chapter 12

- **LESSON 28** Homework - When I'm Old.....

- **POP QUIZ #2** (Pocket Folder)

- **LESSONS 31 & 32** Notes and Reflections on Chapter 13

- **LESSON 32** Homework - Optimist or Pessimist?

- **LESSONS 33 & 34** Notes and Reflections on Chapter 14

- **LESSON 34** Homework - Who to Pick Letter

- **LESSONS 35 & 36** Notes and Reflections on Chapter 15

- **LESSON 36** Homework - Happiness-producing vs. Bad News Processes

- **LESSONS 37 & 38** Notes and Reflections on Chapter 16

- **LESSONS 39 & 40** Notes and Reflections on Chapter 17

- **LESSONS 41 & 42** Notes and Reflections on Chapter 18

LESSON 50 // JOURNEY CHECKLIST #2 cont.

- **LESSONS 43 & 44** Notes from role-playing exercise

- **POP QUIZ #3** (Pocket Folder)

- **LESSON 46** Reflections on Chapter 19

- **LESSONS 47 & 48** Notes and Reflections on Chapter 20

- **LESSON 48** Homework - Cognitive Dissonance

- **LESSONS 49 & 50** Notes on Chapter 21

INITIAL/DATE COMPLETE _____/_____

POINTS OUT OF 50_____

LESSON 51

JOURNEY WORKBOOK/POCKET FOLDER CHECK. Have them work in pairs and check each other. Walk around, spot check, and record points out of 50 possible.

EXPECTATIONS FOR NOTE-TAKING.

READ ALOUD TOGETHER CHAPTER 22, *TOO SOON OLD, TOO LATE SMART*

Love is never lost, not even in death.

POINTS FOR DISCUSSION

1. Grief teaches us about the fragility of life and the finality of death. (p. 115)

2. To lose that which means the most to us is a lesson in helplessness and humility and survival. (p. 115)

3. We ask the inevitable questions, namely 'why me?' and 'why my son?' Really, the question worth contemplating is 'WHAT IS LEFT?' (p. 116)

4. The word "closure" implies that grief is a time-limited process from which we all recover. Not so. It's not about closure.... (p. 116)

5. There is no way around grief - you simply have to go through it. (p. 116)

6. Words - our own and those of others - are all we have to frame the experience, first the despair and then the fragile belief that life still has meaning. (p. 117)

7. THIS IS WHAT PASSES FOR HOPE: THOSE WE HAVE LOST EVOKED IN US FEELINGS OF LOVE THAT WE DIDN'T KNOW WE WERE CAPABLE OF. IT IS OUR TASK TO TRANSFER THAT LOVE TO THOSE WHO STILL NEED US. IN THIS WAY, WE ARE FAITHFUL TO THEIR MEMORIES. (p. 117)

8. Memory and devotion - two ways love overcomes death; through the exercise of memory and devotion, your heart - though broken - will be full and you will stay in the fight to the very last. (p. 118)

LESSON 51 cont.

See where you go with a discussion on grief. This is a tender topic and there should be no pressure to speak up. Perhaps you have a personal experience to share. Bring up compassion. Focus on the 'what is left?' question, and the role of memory and devotion, how we honor and keep the person we lost alive.

NOTES:

....

....

....

....

....

....

....

....

....

....

....

....

....

....

....

....

....

....

LESSON 52

ANY MORE DISCUSSION on grief? Points 1-8 complete?

EXPECTATIONS FOR NOTE-TAKING.

READ ALOUD TOGETHER CHAPTER 23, *TOO SOON OLD, TOO LATE SMART*
Nobody likes to be told what to do.

POINTS FOR DISCUSSION

1. It seems so obvious and yet look how much that passes for intimate communication involves admonitions and instructions!! (p. 119)

2. How many of your interactions involve criticism or directions (the latter being a variation on the former)? (p. 119)

3. When we are told what to do, our most common reaction is resentment progressing to obstinacy. Our refusal can be overt ("not going to do it") or passive-aggressive ("I forgot"), and either way we get frustration all around. (p. 120)

4. OUR DESIRE FOR CONTROL AND A BELIEF THAT WE KNOW HOW THINGS SHOULD BE OVERCOMES OUR COMMON SENSE ABOUT HOW PEOPLE REACT TO ORDERS. (p. 120)

5. What happens around you when you withhold criticism? Some people "awfulize" and think the world will come undone. What happens if you stop the power struggle? How does the atmosphere change? (p. 120)

6. If you expect 'terrible twos' and problems during adolescence, your expectations will likely be realized. (p. 121)

7. If you believe the primary task of parenthood is to shape your children's behavior through constant instruction and the application of rules and punishments, you will likely produce oppositional children who grow into oppositional adults. (p. 121)

8. Passive resistance is the last refuge of the powerless: assembly line workers slow down; children stop doing what they're told, perform poorly in school, ignore instructions, don't

LESSON 52 cont.

do chores, etc., to which parents often respond with even more lectures, instructions, and punishments. (p. 121-122)

9. Question for parents: do you really think your children don't get it? Or is the problem in the repetitive, critical nature of the relationship? (p. 122)

10. Because judgmental people were generally raised in judgmental families, they find it hard to interact another way. It is easier to keep doing what we're used to even if it is evidently not working for us. (p. 123)

11. The idea that it is possible to live without criticizing and directing everyone around us is a novel one for many people. (p. 123)

12. Many parents are caught up in the idea that we have to teach our children everything they need to succeed; many parents are afraid they are not up to the task, afraid they will fail and their children will be lost, and in our efforts to be good teachers, all we transmit is our anxiety, uncertainty, and fear of failure! (p. 123-124)

13. THE PRIMARY GOAL OF PARENTING, BEYOND KEEPING OUR CHILDREN SAFE AND LOVED, IS TO CONVEY TO THEM A SENSE THAT IT IS POSSIBLE TO BE HAPPY IN AN UNCERTAIN WORLD, TO GIVE THEM HOPE. (p. 124)

14. <u>WE DO THIS BY EXAMPLE</u> more than by anything we say to them. If we demonstrate in our own lives the qualities of commitment, determination, and optimism, then we have done our job. (p. 124)

15. We cannot expect that children who are constantly criticized, bullied, and lectured will think well of themselves and their futures. (p. 124)

LESSON 53

EXPECTATIONS FOR NOTE-TAKING.

REVIEW AND FINISH DISCUSSION on Lesson 52, points 1-15. Reiterate the point: people don't like being told what to do. And particularly reinforce the idea that the primary goal of parenting (beyond safety and love) is to convey to their children a sense that it is possible to be happy in an uncertain world, to give them hope. The best way to convey this message, again, is by example. You get what you give so pay attention to what you give.

HOMEWORK

Go to Lesson 53 Homework in the Journey Workbook, explain directions. Use class time to begin, tomorrow will also be a work period.

Due in 2 days, 50 points.

NOTES:

....

....

....

....

....

....

....

....

....

....

....

....

....

....

LESSON 53 // HOMEWORK

LETTER ABOUT CRITICISM OR GRATITUDE
Due in 2 days, 50 points.

OPTION 1: CRITICISM
Think about your life. Is there a person who consistently criticizes you or tells you what to do? Write a letter to this person describing the dynamic, how it makes you feel, and what would work better going forward. Be mindful of your wording, avoid blaming, and really stick to your experience so you will be heard and understood. Because your goal is to improve the relationship, I'm looking for how you express the problem, the honesty of your emotions, your openness to looking at your own behavior, and your commitment to resolving the problem.

OPTION 2: GRATITUDE
Think about your life. Is there a person who consistently praises you? Write a letter of gratitude to this person giving some examples of what he/she does, how it makes you feel, and the effect his/her praise has on you. Describe what you are learning from this person and why it matters.

P.S. Sending the letter is optional.

P.P.S. Suggest that your students consider cultivating a daily gratitude practice, either by talking, writing, or thinking about gratitude. Find something to feel grateful for each day..... it's all part of pursuing happiness.

LESSON 53 // HOMEWORK cont.

LETTER ABOUT CRITICISM OR GRATITUDE HOMEWORK SAMPLE
OPTION 1: LETTER ABOUT CRITICISM

Dear Girlfriend,

This is a tough letter to write, but I've given it a lot of thought and decided to go ahead and write it because our relationship is important to me. It is my hope that it will bring us closer and more respectful of each other if I tell you what's on my mind.

Every now and then, when I talk about this other important friend of mine (whom you know), it feels weird when you either make a negative comment about her or you completely change the subject. I'm not sure why this happens. I hope you don't feel threatened by my other friends, and her in particular, because I really love our friendship, and I'm NOT comparing you to my other friends. I think it's good for us both to have other friends, and understand that we relate differently and share different things with different people. It makes things interesting. I'm not going to stop talking about other people or things going on because that feels awkward, like you're controlling me.

Can you please help me understand what's going on? I want you to know I really value our friendship, and I also want to feel comfortable talking about other people or activities going on in my life. Let me know what you think so we can work on fixing this before it becomes a big issue.

Your Friend,

LESSON 53 // HOMEWORK cont.

LETTER ABOUT CRITICISM OR GRATITUDE HOMEWORK SAMPLE
OPTION 2: LETTER ABOUT GRATITUDE

Dear Miss Smith,

You might not remember me because it has been over 30 years, but I attended Tope Elementary for grades 1-6 and you were the principal at the time. When I think back over important people who influenced me, you are on the list.

Those six years of school are very important ones, and a big reason I loved school so much was because you were there everyday, taking charge. I remember being a little afraid of you and hoping I never got in trouble, and thinking you always looked pretty. Even though you were strict, you were also kind and you smiled and laughed too.

You were in charge of the spelling bees and I always tried out and worked hard. I give you a lot of credit for my spelling ability. You were patient and supportive, and helpful when I made a mistake. You made me feel good about myself for trying, and helped me believe I could do even better.

The one time I got in trouble, you were very fair. You listened to me and didn't get mad, and told me that you knew I knew better. I did something stupid, but you still believed I was a good person. How you handled that left a lasting impression.

Your example taught me about fairness, respect, patience, and kindness. You taught me that school is a good place, and being a good student and person is important. You're part of the reason I went into teaching - and I loved it - and probably even part of the reason my sons are great learners and enjoy school. I'm passing it on as best I can!

So thank you for doing your job the way you did and for being such a kind, strong human being who truly believed in children and learning.

With Gratitude,

LESSON 54

REVIEW THE HOMEWORK ASSIGNMENT from yesterday to be sure it is clear. Students have a choice to write a letter of gratitude or a letter to someone who is consistently critical. In either case, students should show how the person has influenced him/her, give examples, and in the latter case, make some suggestions to improve the relationship.

USE THE ENTIRE CLASS to work on the assignment. Walk around the classroom, checking in with each student to hear their topics and ideas. Find out who intends to mail their letter.

HOMEWORK

Finish your letter.

Due tomorrow, 50 points.

NOTES:

....

....

....

....

....

....

....

....

....

....

....

....

....

....

LESSON 55

COLLECT HOMEWORK. In grading, be sure to write comments on a separate sheet so the letter can be mailed, if desired. Have the students who mail their letters keep you posted on what happens.

EXPECTATIONS FOR NOTE-TAKING.

READ ALOUD TOGETHER CHAPTER 24, *TOO SOON OLD, TOO LATE SMART*
    The major advantage of illness is that it provides relief from responsibility.

POINTS FOR DISCUSSION

1. People seeking psychotherapy are generally in pain and need help, so it is interesting to ask: Do your present difficulties present any advantages? Is there some sort of payoff associated with being depressed or anxious? (p. 125-126)

2. Basic rule of animal psychology: if a behavior is reinforced, it will continue; if it isn't, it will extinguish. (p. 126)

3. The same is true of people - we repeatedly do those things that get rewarded. (p. 126)

4. One of the heaviest burdens we carry is that of being responsible for ourselves and those we care for. (p. 126)

5. Sometimes the only relief from numbing routine, jobs we hate, unsatisfying relationships, and being responsible for ourselves and those we care for is to get sick or have some sort of disability because it is one of the few socially acceptable ways of easing the weight of responsibility, if only for a little while. (p. 126)

6. When you are sick, you are told to 'take it easy' - to not get up and do all the tasks we can't stand. So sometimes the disadvantages of reduced functioning and physical pain are counterbalanced by the relief of lowered expectations. Most people resent this implication of secondary gain....but it's hard not to wonder. (p. 126-127)

7. The longer someone is disabled, the greater the chance that the illness will become part of their identity - the way we think of ourselves. This is a dangerous

LESSON 55 cont.

development because it gets into our subconscious mind and is resistant to change. (p. 127)

8. Traditional medicine has failed to promote in people a sense that they are active participants in their healing. We think we are helpless, that healing is something that "happens" to us, and we become more dependent on doctors and pills to treat us. (p. 127-128)

9. While medication is important, there is no substitute for psychotherapy and its goal of translating good intentions into behavioral change. It is an extended educational process and teaches that each person is responsible for the choices he or she makes in the pursuit of happiness. It is an important instrument of transformation. (p. 128)

NOTES:

....

....

....

....

....

....

....

....

....

....

....

....

....

LESSON 56

RETURN GRADED LETTERS with comments on a separate sheet. Again, keep in touch with those who follow through on mailing them.

EXPECTATIONS FOR NOTE-TAKING.

REVIEW AND FINISH DISCUSSION on Lesson 55, points 1-9. Talk about this situation - when can 'being sick' or 'disabled' have secondary benefits? Give examples of how this might play out with either people they know or an imagined situation. Have you ever tried it? Do you know people who have made their 'disability' part of their identity? Describe and explain.

Once again, there is the message of patience and determination in translating good intentions into behavioral change. There is no quick fix and getting 'sick' to avoid taking responsibility for one's life does not do a good thing over time. In fact, over time it can become the new way you look at yourself, complete with lowered expectations, excuses, etc., and create an even bigger hole to climb out of.

DROP A HINT... about a pop quiz... coming soon, like tomorrow!

LESSON 57

PASS OUT THE POP QUIZ on chapters 19-24, briefly explain the expectations for answering the questions, answer any of your students' questions, and remind them to use complete sentences, proper spelling, and correct grammar.

PAY ATTENTION. If everyone finishes the quiz and there is class time left, go over the quiz together. Those who finish early can...

READ CHAPTER 25, *TOO SOON OLD, TOO LATE SMART*
We are afraid of the wrong things.

COLLECT THE POP QUIZZES for grading and to be returned tomorrow. Graded pop quizzes go in the Pocket Folder.

NOTES:

....

....

....

....

....

....

....

....

....

....

....

....

....

....

LESSON 57 // POP QUIZ

POP QUIZ #4 ON CHAPTERS 19-24

50 points

Answer the following questions to the best of your ability. Proper grammar and spelling count. Write on the back, if needed.

1. Define 'hypocrisy' and the problem it causes in us.

2. What negative role can luck and excuses play?

3. What does Dr. Livingston consider to be the ultimate folly?

4. Explain cognitive dissonance.

5. Explain the 'myth of the perfect stranger.'

6. What is an essential part of healthy maturation?

7. What question should we be asking when we are in the throes of grief? What does this question do to our thinking?

8. When we lose someone, what can we do to demonstrate our hope?

9. What is the problem with telling others what to do? What gets set up?

10. Describe a failing of traditional medicine and how psychotherapy deals with this failing.

LESSON 57 // POP QUIZ cont.

POP QUIZ #4 SAMPLE ANSWER KEY

1. Hypocrisy is the pretense of having some desirable or publicly-approved attitude or a virtuous character that you don't really possess. It causes a problem because our actions don't line up with our words, and over time this erodes our sense of ourselves. Hypocrisy also erodes trust.

2. Saying that most of what happens to us is luck is an act of laziness. Excuses allow us to avoid taking responsibility. Luck and excuses are a way to avoid the hard work of self-examination.

3. The ultimate folly is to lie to ourselves for temporary comfort because, sooner or later, all the lies on which we then make life decisions are not based in reality and create unhappiness.

4. Cognitive dissonance is when our thoughts go against our feelings and actions. We're out of alignment. We're not authentic. We don't make much sense.

5. The myth of the perfect stranger is the idea that there is a person out there who will save us with his/her love. It starts when we feel dissatisfied with who we're with and wonder what we're missing.

6. Healthy maturation allows us to internalize a belief that we are uniquely valuable and gives us a stable sense of a lovable self.

7. Instead of asking "why me?" we should ask "what's left?" because that shifts our focus back to living. Death is inevitable and tragic things happen, and we must go on living for those who still need us.

8. We can demonstrate our hope by transferring all the love we had for the lost person to those who still need us. In this way, we are faithful to their memories.

9. Being told what to do feels bad, we resent it, and it sets up a situation where people

LESSON 57 // POP QUIZ cont.

get stubborn, there's a power struggle, which often brings on even more criticism and directions!!

10. Traditional medicine leads us to believe we can pop a pill and feel better, and that healing "happens" to us. It fails to show that we are an active participant in our healing. Therapy is an extended educational process in which we take charge of our healing by learning to translate good intentions into behavioral change. We are responsible for our happiness.

NOTES:

....

....

....

....

....

....

....

....

....

....

....

....

....

....

....

....

....

OVERVIEW

LESSONS 58-75

TOO SOON OLD, TOO LATE SMART CHAPTERS

25   We are afraid of the wrong things.

26   Parents have a limited ability to shape children's behavior, except for the worse.

27   The only real paradises are those we have lost.

28   Of all the forms of courage, the ability to laugh is the most profoundly therapeutic.

29   Mental health requires freedom of choice.

30   Forgiveness is a form of letting go, but they are not the same thing.

HOMEWORK ASSIGNMENTS (6) + samples
- 100 Words on Meditation
- Role Models
- Eulogy
- Jokes
- Survival Strategies Poster
- Epitaph

POP QUIZ #5 ON CHAPTERS 25-30

LESSON 58

RETURN GRADED POP QUIZZES. Any questions? Keep in Pocket Folder.

EXPECTATIONS FOR NOTE-TAKING.

READ ALOUD TOGETHER CHAPTER 25, *TOO SOON OLD, TOO LATE SMART*
We are afraid of the wrong things.

POINTS FOR DISCUSSION

1. We live in a fear-promoting society, with advertising and the news being big drivers, stoking our anxieties about what we have, what we look like, and whether we're sexually adequate. (p. 129) Talk about examples.

2. ONE OF THE THINGS THAT DEFINES US IS WHAT WE WORRY ABOUT. Life is full of uncertainty and random catastrophe so we can justify almost any anxiety. (p. 130)

3. PHOBIA - an irrational and disabling fear. (p. 130)

4. Interesting that the real risks to our welfare - smoking, over-eating, not fastening seat belts, social injustice, and the people we elect to office - provoke little anxiety. (p. 131)

5. Just as a phobia can distract us from loneliness, as a nation we can use mad cow disease, killer bees, or prowlers in the night to distract us from global warming or environmental degradation or other problems that seem beyond our individual ability to influence. (p. 131)

6. Our relations with each other are characterized by mistrust. Instead of a sense of shared fate and that we can all prosper, we often behave like life is a competition to be won at the expense of others. (p. 131)

7. Look at the legal system and frivolous lawsuits. Discuss Dr. Livingston's idea of a "misfortune fund." The money collected from punishing corporations for outrageous negligence could go to a fund for people facing extraordinary expenses that were no one's fault. This would reinforce the idea that we all share in the inevitable uncertainties and risks that are a part of life. (p. 132)

LESSON 58 cont.

8. Being compensated for economic loss is one thing, but no amount of money can - or should - make up for the random suffering that is our common fate. (p. 132)

9. When we see people who have succeeded with little or no effort - trust fund babies, winning the lottery, no-talent entertainers - this can lead to a distorted sense of what is valuable or lasting...and our own lives and relationships seem boring by comparison. (p. 133)

10. Though unpleasant to experience, fear can be an adaptive emotion if it results in actions that protect us from harm. The threats must be identified realistically, which requires accurate information and an ability to integrate it into useful knowledge. This is challenging when our sources of information have a stake in keeping us afraid. (p. 133)

11. We do a similar thing in our personal lives - much of what we do is driven by the fear of failure. For example, we go after material wealth like it is the ultimate prize and are distracted from the activities and people that provide more lasting pleasure and satisfaction. (p. 134)

12. Much of our behavior is driven by some combination of greed and competition; the successful entrepreneur is the model of the American success story, but the quality or usefulness of the work is insignificant compared to the wealth it generates. (p. 134)

13. Fear can be effective in the short-term, but it is not useful in producing lasting change because it ignores our powerful desire to pursue happiness and gain self-respect. Better jobs, education, the chance to improve one's life, and a sense of fairness and opportunity lead to lasting satisfaction. (p. 134-135)

14. Learn to savor the moments of pleasure that our brief lives contain. This takes courage and a resolve to not let the present moment be drained of joy by fear of the future or regret for the past. (p. 135)

BE PRESENT......

LESSON 59 // MEDITATION

EXPECTATIONS FOR NOTE-TAKING.

REVIEW AND FINISH DISCUSSION on Lesson 58, points 1-14. Talk about the media and advertising and how they promote our fears. Who do you trust? Who and what are reliable sources of information? Talk about the importance of asking questions and thinking critically.

Talk about random uncertainty and the role it plays in our lives. How can random uncertainty teach us to be more present and appreciative?

Talk about mindfulness and paying attention. Discuss the kinds of activities that are reflective, about noticing what's going on in our minds, strengthening our connection to ourselves, like writing in a journal, doing yoga, or meditating.

Do a 3-5 MINUTE BREATHING MEDITATION with your students. Have them get into a comfortable seated position at their desk or perhaps there is an area on the floor that would work. Hands rest on their thighs or knees, eyes are closed. Tell them to just follow their breath, inhaling and exhaling, and watch what the mind does. Meditation-type music is an option or silence - the point is to practice paying attention to what's going on in their minds. Slowly bring them back to the present. Share what happened.

HOMEWORK

Go to Lesson 59 Homework in the Journey Workbook, explain directions. Answer questions. At home tonight, meditate first and then write about it.

Due tomorrow, 50 points.

LESSON 59 // HOMEWORK

100 WORDS ON MEDITATION

Due tomorrow, 50 points.

- Find a quiet place where you won't be disturbed.
- Meditation-type music is an option. Light a candle if you want. Create a calm, relaxing atmosphere.
- Shoes off. Comfortable clothing.
- Get into a comfortable position either seated or lying on your back on the floor. If you choose a seated position and have tight hips, sitting on a pillow, a block, or a big dictionary helps. Be smart about the position you pick because you're going to be in it for 15 minutes....don't fall asleep! A family member can be your timer.
- Close your eyes and slowly bring your attention to your breath, inhaling and exhaling. Notice when your mind wanders away from your breath and bring it back to that single point of attention, the breath. Notice what thoughts come up and how you "talk" to yourself. Notice if you are patient. Notice how still you are. Watch your mind and focus on your breath.
- In 100 words minimum, write about the experience.

LESSON 59 // HOMEWORK cont.

100 WORDS ON MEDITATION HOMEWORK SAMPLE

I've been practicing yoga for many years now. Yoga is often called a moving meditation, as opposed to a seated meditation, and both are a practice of looking at and calming the mind by following the breath. In the beginning, I remember it being very challenging to only pay attention to my breathing - my thoughts would interfere with trying to only pay attention to my inhales and exhales. I'd think about the errands I had to run or what I'd fix for dinner or my sons' busy schedules. I would also have reactions to my thoughts, like frustration or impatience about everything that needed to be done. Or I'd hear a self-critical voice telling me all the ways I could do a better job. It felt like my mind was running at high idle and it wasn't very relaxing or joyful. It was mostly about doing instead of being.

Eventually, with practice, I could go longer stretches focusing on my breathing before a thought would arise. Meditation is not about stopping your thinking - it's about becoming calmer, less reactive, and less attached to our thoughts. Staying with my breath, I learned to create some space between myself and my thoughts so I could just notice them, and not judge or react to them. While meditating, it helped to think of my thoughts as clouds floating across the sky.

All these years later, my mind is calmer, less reactive, more responsive - I am better at directing my thinking. Round-and-round thinking wears a person out. I'm more about slowing down and appreciating, not taking things too personally. But it is an ongoing practice - if I get lazy, my mind will go back to its old tricks.

LESSON 60

COLLECT HOMEWORK and spend a few minutes talking about meditating. Did you like it? Will you continue? What was hard about it? Encourage a daily reflective activity.

EXPECTATIONS FOR NOTE-TAKING.

READ ALOUD TOGETHER CHAPTER 26, *TOO SOON OLD, TOO LATE SMART*
  Parents have a limited ability to shape children's behavior, except for the worse.

POINTS FOR DISCUSSION

1. For parents to think that we are solely, or even primarily, responsible for the successes and failures of our children is a narcissistic myth. (p. 137)

2. The job of parents is to love their children and to provide a stable, nurturing environment for them to grow. Beyond that, our children succeed or fail primarily because of their own good or bad decisions about how they will live their lives. (p. 137)

3. Parents can try to teach the values and behaviors they have found to be important, but IT IS THE WAY WE LIVE AS ADULTS THAT CONVEYS THE REAL MESSAGE TO OUR CHILDREN ABOUT WHAT WE BELIEVE IN. WHETHER THEY CHOOSE TO INTEGRATE THESE VALUES INTO THEIR OWN LIVES IS UP TO THEM. (p. 137-138)

4. Kids have a nose for hypocrisy. If there are major contradictions between what we say and what we do, our children are likely to notice and be cynical, but ultimately, as independent human beings, they bear the responsibility for how they incorporate what they saw or learned in childhood. There is an expiration date on blaming your parents! (p. 138)

5. Anxiety is contagious. At an early age, children can sense it; new parents worry about 'doing it right.' (p. 138)

6. There are many different ideas about discipline ranging from rigid/controlling to permissive. There is an expectation that child rearing is a series of power struggles that the parents must win and that it is perfectly legitimate to use one's greater psychological and physical size to ensure victory. (p. 139)

LESSON 60 cont.

7. Consider adopting a less rigid, more optimistic method of discipline grounded in the idea that, with love and support, most children grow into happy, productive adults: set reasonable limits on children's behavior so that less confrontation and resentment is provoked. (p. 139)

8. Success in parenting is not about being right and having all the answers - it is about establishing limits and loving and respecting your kids. (p. 140)

9. Too much exercising authority over meaningless things ultimately leads to resentment and passive-aggressive resistance, e.g. food consumption and room cleanliness. (p. 140)

10. Children raised in homes where parental control is severe turn out to have a poor set of internalized limits because they have experienced only rigid external rules. Conversely, children growing up with few constraints do not have a way to learn those guidelines necessary to live comfortably with others. (p. 140-141)

11. OUR PRIMARY TASK AS PARENTS, BEYOND ATTENDING TO THE DAY-TO-DAY PHYSICAL AND EMOTIONAL WELFARE OF OUR CHILDREN, IS TO CONVEY TO THEM A SENSE THAT THEY CAN BE HAPPY IN AN UNCERTAIN AND IMPERFECT WORLD. WE CAN ONLY ACCOMPLISH THIS BY EXAMPLE. (p. 141)

12. It is infinitely discouraging to encounter a pessimistic young person who has already decided that life holds little prospect of turning out well. Where did they learn this??? (p. 142)

13. It is easy to be cynical and always find something negative about the world - it's amazing we're not all depressed! How can anyone be happy in such a world? (p. 142)

14. The answer lies in SELECTIVE ATTENTION: if we choose to focus our awareness and energy on those things and people that bring us pleasure and satisfaction, we have a very good chance of being happy in a world full of unhappiness. You become what you pay attention to. (p. 142)

LESSON 60 cont.

15. It is the ultimate demonstration of courage to bring ourselves, even momentarily, to enjoy life even as we are surrounded by evidence of its brevity and potential for disaster. (p. 143)

16. The ability to do this, to be happy with each other, constitutes the most useful example we can provide our children. (p. 143)

17. A sense of humor helps, too! (p. 143)

RECOMMENDED: Practice meditating for 10 minutes.

LESSON 61

Did anyone PRACTICE MEDITATING last night? How did it go?

EXPECTATIONS FOR NOTE-TAKING.

REVIEW AND FINISH DISCUSSION on Lesson 60, points 1-17. Segue into a discussion about parenting and role models. Have them LIST THE ATTRIBUTES of an effective role model - "walking the talk" should be on the list. REVIEW THE DEFINITION of 'hypocrisy' - a pretense of having desirable or publicly-approved attitudes, saying one thing and doing another.

TALK ABOUT RESPONSIBILITY and how it is ultimately up to us how we incorporate what we learned and saw in childhood. If we saw hypocrisy, we can choose to repeat that and become hypocritical or we can learn to model the positive behaviors and values we want to teach others. If we learned to live with severe parental control, we can choose to grow up and be controlling or we can overcome this by learning to internalize limits and trust ourselves to live comfortably within them. If we saw pessimism at every turn, we can choose to perpetuate that pessimistic attitude or we can learn to be more optimistic.

Being happy and healthy depends in large part on recognizing our choices.

HOMEWORK
Go to Lesson 61 in the Journey Workbook, explain directions.
Due tomorrow, one page, 50 points.

RECOMMENDED: Practice meditating for 10 minutes.

LESSON 61 // HOMEWORK

ROLE MODELS

Due tomorrow, one page, 50 points.

Think about your parents and the type of role models they are. What are the positive things you are learning from them, the things you want to carry forward into a relationship and to, one day, being a parent? What are you learning that you may not want to repeat as an adult in a relationship and also, one day, as a parent? Is there a dynamic that drives you crazy? Remember, no one is perfect, including our parents. You may not give it much attention, but you are benefitting in many ways from your parents. It is important to be aware of what you are learning from them and how you want to incorporate that into your adult life and relationships.

RECOMMENDED: Practice meditating for 10-15 minutes.

LESSON 61 // HOMEWORK cont.

ROLE MODELS HOMEWORK SAMPLE

Growing up was mostly a positive experience for me. My parents loved, supported, and nurtured me each in their own way. My mom took care of me, fed us great meals, kept a clean house, worked hard, was active in the community, and was always at all my volleyball and basketball games. She was a great role model for being loving, patient, and affectionate. She encouraged me to do my best. She took care of things and took pride in raising her three kids. I learned a lot from her about making a home feel like home, and I take great pride and joy in being a mom now. One thing that I've had to work through is my mom's occasional lack of communication about her emotions. When her words didn't match her emotion, I got confused, like saying "fine" when it really wasn't. It made it hard for me to read or understand what was really going on. Today I try to be a consistent and clear role model for expressing what I'm feeling so my actions and words make sense. I'm pretty good at explaining why I'm feeling what I'm feeling because it's important to me to not be confusing to my own kids.

My dad was a solid role model for working hard and getting a great education. He placed high value on learning. So I learned to be an excellent student and love learning. My dad didn't talk about emotions so from him I learned to be rational and serious. His thing was to not say much and leave it to me to figure things out by his example, which was difficult when there wasn't much feedback. It was hard to tell if he was proud of me. A little feedback would have been helpful. So with my kids, starting when they were younger, I gave them feedback. I modeled the behaviors I wanted them to learn AND I offered an explanation, when appropriate. Now that they're older, they "get it" and just don't need much explanation.

So I've taken my mom and dad's role modeling, made a few changes, rounded it out with more complete communication, and I've found what works for me. Because I have a flexible mindset, I can make adjustments in my parenting style as my kids need me less and find their own way. They have a solid map to work from, and they know I love them because my words and actions are congruous.

LESSON 62

COLLECT HOMEWORK essays on role-modeling. What did you learn? Is there a particular behavior pattern that you're going to pay more attention to?

How many of you MEDITATED? How did it go?

EXPECTATIONS FOR NOTE-TAKING.

READ ALOUD TOGETHER CHAPTER 27, *TOO SOON OLD, TOO LATE SMART*
        The only real paradises are those we have lost.

POINTS FOR DISCUSSION

1. DEFINE 'NOSTALGIA' - a wistful desire to return in thought or in fact to a former time in one's life.

2. When people speak about the way things used to be, it is almost always in contrast to what is happening now, and can reflect a kind of gloom about the future....and in our selective memories, things were always better, less expensive, and simpler in the past. (p. 144)

3. Things were not really better long ago. Examples: infectious diseases, wars, crime, poverty were all present....and people weren't, on balance, more virtuous. (p. 145)

4. We long for the security provided by the comforting illusions of our youth (the breathless infatuation of first love), and we regret the complications imposed by our mistakes, the compromises of our integrity, the roads not taken. The cumulative weight of our imperfect lives is harder to bear as we weaken in body and spirit. (p. 145)

5. Eulogies can sanitize a life. TO KNOW SOMEONE FULLY AND LOVE THEM IN SPITE OF, EVEN BECAUSE OF, THEIR IMPERFECTIONS IS AN ACT THAT REQUIRES US TO RECOGNIZE AND FORGIVE, TWO VERY IMPORTANT INDICATORS OF EMOTIONAL MATURITY. Do this for others and do it for yourself too!! (p. 146)

6. It is our fallibility and uncertainty that make us human. It's not about seeking perfection, which is unattainable; it is about finding ways to be happy in an imperfect world. Clinging to an idealized vision of the past pretty much insures dissatisfaction with the present. (p. 146)

7. What is memory? It is not an accurate transcription of the past, but rather the story we

LESSON 62 cont.

tell ourselves about the past that is full of distortions, wishful thinking, and unfulfilled dreams. Example: How can people recall shared events so differently? (p. 146-147)

8. What we remember and how we remember it are affected by the meaning and effort we are using to construct a coherent narrative of our lives that reflects what we think of ourselves and how we became the people we are - or wish we were. (p. 147)

9. For example, siblings often have distinctly different recollections of their upbringing even when raised in the same house by the same parents. One sibling remembers abuse while another denies it. (p. 147)

10. We don't like to revise our personal mythologies - we have absorbed the notion that our destinies are shaped by our childhood experience, and we stay stuck blaming our parents, or we idealize, or we can't forget 'the one that got away.' This can make it hard to risk our hearts again. (p. 147-148)

11. The problem with longing for the past is that it distracts us from our efforts to find pleasure and meaning in the present. (p. 148)

12. The good news is that life expectancy is increasing; the bad news is that the extra years are tacked on at the end! (p. 149)

13. We all have latitude in how we interpret our own histories. We have the power to idealize or denigrate the people in our lives, we can color our pasts happy or sad. It depends on our current need to see ourselves a certain way. (p. 150)

14. As we get older, we face the choice of accepting and enjoying what we have made of our lives. Some people turn to religion. Some people surrender to the unknown. Either way, we long for meaning. We can become cynical and wish to regain what once was, or we can stay hopeful all the way to the western horizon. (p. 150)

RECOMMENDED: Practice meditating for 10-15 minutes. Refer to guidelines from Lesson 59, if necessary.

LESSON 63

How many of you PRACTICED MEDITATING last night? How did it go?

EXPECTATIONS FOR NOTE-TAKING.

REVIEW AND FINISH DISCUSSION on Lesson 62, points 1-14. The main message here is to stay present because if we spend too much time longing for the past, thinking it was so much better than now, we lose our ability to be happy in the present. We have a choice both in how we remember our lives and how we accept and enjoy what we've made of them, and in how we carry our story into the future. If you attend family reunions, think about what goes on there. Share some stories. Ask about their grandparents and how they, the grandparents, remember their lives. Have any of your students been to a memorial service? Ask: how do you want to both remember and be remembered?

HOMEWORK

Go to Lesson 63 Homework in the Journey Workbook, explain directions.
Due tomorrow, 50 points.

RECOMMENDED: Practice meditating for 10-15 minutes.

NOTES:

....

....

....

....

....

....

....

....

....

....

LESSON 63 // HOMEWORK

EULOGY

Due tomorrow, 50 points.

In one typed page, write your own eulogy. How do you want to be remembered? How do you think others will remember you? Feel free to have a conversation with and get the perspective of a parent about this assignment.

NOTES:

....

....

....

....

....

....

....

....

....

....

....

....

....

....

....

....

....

LESSON 63 // HOMEWORK cont.

EULOGY HOMEWORK SAMPLE

It is my hope that, as you gather in my memory, you will remember me as I was and not as some idealized version of me - I didn't want to be perfect, really, in spite of occasional, foolish attempts. I was just me. Imperfect, occasionally uncertain, sometimes too serious and earnest, and yet striving to be happy and do a good job nevertheless. My parents were great and taught me a lot of important things. I had the two best brothers ever. I loved learning all the way to the end. It mattered to me to be healthy so I loved sports growing up and stayed active all my life. I especially loved being outside and the surprises and beauty of the natural world. I loved chocolate and my perfect nespresso lattes.

It took a few decades, four to be precise, before I did my great pulling-it-all-together and, after that, my life had a depth and meaning that could bring tears to my eyes. So many things - sitting on the porch swing with a best friend, laughing with my boys, the sky, my faithful Chugs, the smell of fresh-cut hay and coffee beans and a crisp fall morning, the sound of mountain water and sand hill cranes, tall sunflowers, fresh-tilled soil, chocolate chip cookies, dancing....all of it warmed my heart and kept me light on my feet, grateful, present. Then, when my big brother died much too young of brain cancer, my world lost all color, everything changed, and I mourned and grieved my way back to the fragile belief that my life still had meaning. I took care of what was left and I missed him all the rest of my days. I hope we're together now.

Really it was my relationships with people that made my life hum. I learned much about what I had to offer by opening myself up to others. Surely one of my greatest joys was being a mom to my sons, two of the most remarkable young men on the planet. And certainly experiencing the love of my life was beyond any notion I had of the enabling, expansive, renewing quality of love. I shared my whole, adoring heart, and felt safe. He loved me in all my emotions and wrapped me in an ease that blankets me still. We had so much fun together.

I like to think that I worked out most of my kinks and spent the latter part of my life truly enjoying being alive, more empathetic with how we all struggle, more relaxed and confident, laughing and smiling more, seeing the good in others, the hope. Life is such a gift. Thank you for being part of mine. I hope I made your lives even a little bit brighter and that you carry a sweet memory of me. I gave it my all and I did my imperfect best.....and as you carry on, remember me when you drink a margarita. Remember to go for it, and go ahead and dance like no one is watching! And yes, I am smiling.

LESSON 64

Spend this class period SHARING EULOGIES. Create a supportive environment, let them know it is optional to read what they wrote. After each student reads, ask the class if they have any additional positive feedback. We often don't see ourselves clearly and others might bring an interesting insight to light, a positive element that we weren't even aware we were showing, but that others have experienced in us.

How many of you talked to a parent about the assignment and how did that go?

How many of you PRACTICED MEDITATING - or did some form of CONTEMPLATIVE ACTIVITY? Do you notice yourself feeling calmer and more centered? Ask for examples. Again, you may have to go first with an example from your everyday life.

RECOMMENDED: Practice meditating - or do some form of contemplative activity like journal writing or yoga or listening to music - for 10-15 minutes.

NOTES:

....

....

....

....

....

....

....

....

....

....

....

....

LESSON 65

How many of you PRACTICED MEDITATING, or journal writing, again last night?

EXPECTATIONS FOR NOTE-TAKING.

READ ALOUD TOGETHER CHAPTER 28, *TOO SOON OLD, TOO LATE SMART*

   Of all the forms of courage, the ability to laugh is the most profoundly therapeutic.

POINTS FOR DISCUSSION

1.   DEFINE 'AMBIVALENCE' - the psychological definition is "the coexistence within an individual of positive and negative feelings toward the same person, object, or action, simultaneously drawing him or her in opposite directions."

2.   It is hard to feel two opposite emotions at the same time - we either feel one thing or the other. For example, the antidote for anxious people is deep muscle relaxation. If they learn how to relax their muscles, they have a tool they can use when they are feeling anxious. (p. 152)

3.   Standard components of anxiety or a panic attack - rapid heartbeat, hyperventilation, sweating, and a sense of doom. (p. 152)

4.   Depressed people rarely - if ever - laugh and yet they often think they have a good sense of humor! You can't laugh and be depressed at the same time. (p. 153)

5.   SO WHY IS LAUGHTER SO IMPORTANT IN OUR LIVES? BECAUSE IT IS A SIGNIFICANT COMPONENT, AND INDICATOR, OF A HAPPY LIFE. (p. 153)

6.   Many people are so unaccustomed to finding anything funny that they have lost the capacity for SURPRISE, which is the essence of humor. (p. 154)

7.   What gives humor its power in our lives is that a capacity for laughter is one of the two characteristics that separate us from other animals; the other, as far as we know, is the ability to contemplate our own death. (p. 154)

8.   These two uniquely human attributes cut to the heart of the great paradox of life: IT IS POSSIBLE TO BE HAPPY IN THE FACE OF OUR MORTALITY. To laugh at ourselves is

LESSON 65 cont.

to acknowledge the ultimate futility of our efforts to stave off the depredations of time. (p. 154)

9.   "Gallows humor" - laughter in the face of death. We are in the grip of forces we can't control (i.e. we're all going to die), but we still don't give up and we can always laugh. TO BE ABLE TO EXPERIENCE FULLY THE SADNESS AND ABSURDITY THAT LIFE SO OFTEN PRESENTS AND STILL FIND REASONS TO GO ON IS AN ACT OF COURAGE ABETTED BY OUR ABILITY TO BOTH LOVE AND LAUGH. (p. 155)

10. Humor heals. The mind/body interplay is at the heart of every theory of how we can influence recovery by the ways in which we think and feel about whatever is happening to us. (p. 155)

11. Humor is a way of sharing....we are all in this lifeboat together. The sea surrounds us, rescue is uncertain, control is illusory...still we sail on - together. (p. 156)

12. Pessimists, like hypochondriacs, are right in the long run - nobody gets out of here alive. But pessimism, like any attitude, contains within it a multitude of self-fulfilling prophecies. If we approach others in a suspicious or hostile way, they are likely to respond accordingly, thereby confirming our low expectations. (p. 156)

13. Fortunately the opposite is also true. HABITUAL OPTIMISM CAN'T PROTECT US FROM OCCASIONAL DISAPPOINTMENT, BUT IT IS BETTER THAN THE ALTERNATIVE. Pessimism is a close cousin of despair. (p. 156)

14. It feels good to smile. Things may be grave, we are indeed going to die one day, but we don't have to be so serious. (p. 157)

RECOMMENDED: Practice meditating for 10-15 minutes.

LESSON 66

Did any of you PRACTICE MEDITATING last night? How did it go?

EXPECTATIONS FOR NOTE-TAKING.

REVIEW AND FINISH DISCUSSION on Lesson 65, points 1-14. Talk about laughter and humor and its therapeutic qualities. Do you laugh every day? Do your parents laugh? Do you laugh with your parents? Ask students to share stories of how laughter/humor turned a potentially bad experience into one that worked out okay. You may have to go first so be prepared!

Humor is something to share, it connects us to others. It can level the field and allow us to show compassion - we are all in this together and eventually we are all going to die. It is indeed grave, but it doesn't have to be serious.

If there is time, have students share some of their favorite childhood jokes. ("Why was 6 afraid of 7? Because 7 8 9." "What did the zero say to the 8? Nice belt." "Why did the seagull fly over the sea? Because if he flew over the bay, he'd be a bagel.")

HOMEWORK
Go to Lesson 66 Homework in the Journey Workbook, explain directions.
Due tomorrow, 50 points.

RECOMMENDED: Practice meditating for 10-15 minutes.

LESSON 66 // HOMEWORK

JOKES!!!

Due tomorrow, 50 points.

Come to class tomorrow prepared to tell two or three G or PG-rated jokes. Memorize them. Practice at home in front of the mirror or willing family members, even the dog! Be prepared to laugh, relax, and have a good time.

NOTES:

....

....

....

....

....

....

....

....

....

....

....

....

....

....

....

....

LESSON 66 / HOMEWORK cont.

JOKES HOMEWORK SAMPLE

EXPENSIVE FISHING TRIP

Two redneck guys go on a fishing trip.

They rent all the gear - reels, rods, waders, rowboat, car, and even a cabin in the woods.

They spend a fortune.

The first day they go fishing, they don't catch anything.

The same thing happens the second and third days.

So it goes until finally on the last day one of them catches a fish.

As they're driving home, they're really depressed. One guy turns to the other and says, "Do you realize that this one lousy fish we caught cost us $1500?"

The other guy says, "Wow! It's a good thing we didn't catch any more!"

BLONDE JOKES

I knew a blonde who was so stupid that.....

....she called me to get my phone number.

....she spent 20 minutes looking at the orange juice box because it said 'concentrate.'

....she tried to put M&Ms in alphabetical order.

....she sent me a fax with a stamp on it.

....she tried to drown a fish.

....she thought a quarterback was a refund.

....she tripped over her cordless phone.

....she asked for a price check at the Dollar Store.

....she studied for a blood test.

....when she missed the 44 bus, she took the 22 bus twice instead.

....she took a ruler to bed to see how long she slept.

LESSON 67

ENJOY THIS CLASS!!!!!

Go around the class and have each student stand and share their jokes. The jokes should be memorized, not read. Relax, laugh out loud, and have fun. Go with the flow without the class getting out of hand.

Wrap up the joke-telling with a reminder about the important healing and connecting power of laughter. Again, it's about reconciling our inevitable mortality with our ability to find humor in the face of our shared fate.

If there is time, ask the students if they have any questions about the class and the topics we have covered. Again, go with the flow, give them some space to offer feedback and share with each other what they are learning in the class, the pace, the reading, the homework load, etc.

RECOMMENDED: Practice meditating for 10-15 minutes.

NOTES:

....

....

....

....

....

....

....

....

....

....

....

LESSON 68

Who PRACTICED MEDITATING last night? How did it go? Keep it up!

EXPECTATIONS FOR NOTE-TAKING.

READ ALOUD TOGETHER CHAPTER 29, *TOO SOON OLD, TOO LATE SMART*
> Mental health requires freedom of choice.

POINTS FOR DISCUSSION

1. Emotional disorders of any form constrain a person in some way; the person must adjust their behavior to compensate for their illness (depression, anxiety, bipolar illness or schizophrenia). (p. 158)

2. Depressed people experience a loss of energy, an inability to concentrate, and a sad mood, and these things cause us to withdraw from the people and activities that previously gave us pleasure. (p. 158-159)

3. When the condition has a biological basis (as with those listed above), medication can be helpful. To the degree that our functioning and relationships are affected, it is important to also take a behavioral approach to treatment. (p. 159)

4. CARDINAL RULE OF ANXIETY: AVOIDANCE MAKES IT WORSE; CONFRONTATION GRADUALLY IMPROVES IT. (p. 159)

5. With depression, the behavior that needs changing involves overcoming the inertia and fatigue enough to do the things that predictably make us feel better. This is a lot to ask when someone is discouraged, pessimistic, and feeling worthless. Get moving, get busy, do the things you know you enjoy. (p. 159)

6. Those who care, day in and day out, for a disabled loved one are seldom recognized for their bravery, patience, and love. (p. 160)

7. It's not about feeling fortunate to have fewer burdens than the next guy; it's about the fact that EVERY LIFE CONTAINS LOSSES - HOW WE RESPOND TO THEM IS WHAT DEFINES US. (p. 160)

LESSON 68 cont.

8. For those who have lost a child, what choice do we have? Should we die and abandon those who still depend on us? Our own death may be preferable to the prospect of life without the lost loved one, but that relief is denied us so we bear what we must and soldier on. (p. 161)

9. MENTAL HEALTH IS A FUNCTION OF CHOICE. The more choices we are able to exercise, the happier we are likely to be. (p. 161)

10. Those who are most unwell or discouraged suffer from a sense that their choices have been limited, sometimes by external circumstances or illness, but most often by the many ways we restrict ourselves. (p. 161)

11. Tolerance of risk is the primary variable here: if we are afraid of change, then it is hard to choose a life that makes us happy. What is really restricting us - is it anxiety or lack of imagination? (p. 161)

12. WE ARE NEVER OUT OF CHOICES no matter how desperate the circumstances. (p. 161)

13. The essence of psychotherapy is to empathize with the burdens people bear without giving in to despair and to always convey the conviction that all is not lost. (p. 161)

WE ARE NOT DEAD YET............

RECOMMENDED: Practice meditating for 10-15 minutes.

LESSON 69

WHO PRACTICED MEDITATING? How is it going? Do you notice any benefits? For those of you who aren't practicing, why not?

EXPECTATIONS FOR NOTE-TAKING.

REVIEW AND FINISH DISCUSSION on Lesson 68, points 1-13. The main point to reinforce here is that no matter how bad things seem to be, we always have a choice. If we slide into depression - loss of energy, inability to concentrate, sad mood - we have to overcome the inertia and fatigue and do the things we know bring us pleasure; if we don't, we'll get stuck. Brainstorm strategies that can help us get unstuck and move out of a depressed mood. What activities and people are enjoyable and always help you feel better?

GO TO THE SURVIVAL STRATEGIES POSTER (SSP) project description in the Journey Workbook. Pick a due date one week out and have them write it at the top. Review the assignment. Brainstorm ideas with them, illustrate an idea on the board, answer questions, pass out construction paper. Class time tomorrow to work on it so come prepared. Sample ideas: take a bubble bath; call my best friend; play music and dance; do yoga or go for a run; work in my garden; do something kind for someone else.

HOMEWORK
Start working on your SSP project.
Due in one week, 100 points.

RECOMMENDED: Practice meditating for 10-15 minutes.

LESSON 69 // PROJECT

SURVIVAL STRATEGIES POSTER (SSP)

Due in one week, 100 points.

MATERIALS: construction paper, colored pencils, or markers

Create a poster that lists at least 10 things you can do that will pull you out of a blue mood and get you back on track again. The list will reflect how well you know yourself, your moods, and what works for you. Be creative and colorful and have fun illustrating your poster. Make sure it has a clever title. Use the piece of construction paper, 12 x 18, provided by your teacher. Please do not use a computer on this project unless you have the teacher's okay.

LESSON 70

Who PRACTICED MEDITATING last night and how did it go?

WORK ON SSP. Use the entire class to get them rolling on this assignment. By the end of class, each student should have a complete list of his/her 10 survival strategies. Walk around the room and check in with each student, ask to see his/her list, help them brainstorm. Once their list is complete, have them sketch out a rough draft with their illustration ideas. Remind them to include a title. It's about being honest about what works for you - about how well you know yourself and how to get 'unstuck' - and being creative and colorful in how you illustrate it. Hopefully this is a poster you will place somewhere you frequent, to remind you that you always have choices...... you're not dead yet!

Create a comfortable and productive work environment by engaging and showing your enthusiasm. Consider background music. Connect with each student. Quality and depth of thinking count - push back on their ideas if they seem superficial.

HOMEWORK
Continue work on your SSP.

RECOMMENDED: Practice meditating for 10-15 minutes.

NOTES:

....

....

....

....

....

....

....

....

....

....

LESSON 71

Any MEDITATING still going on?

EXPECTATIONS FOR NOTE-TAKING.

READ ALOUD TOGETHER CHAPTER 30, *TOO SOON OLD, TOO LATE SMART*
Forgiveness is a form of letting go, but they are not the same thing.

POINTS FOR DISCUSSION

1. Life can be seen as a series of relinquishments all leading up to the final letting go of our earthly selves. (p. 162)

2. Why is it so hard to surrender the past? (p. 162)

3. Our memories, good and bad, give us a sense of continuity and link the many people we have been to the one who temporarily inhabits our changing body. (p. 162)

4. When our childhoods aren't ideal, and for most of us they aren't, it is easy to get caught up in self-definitions that involve past traumas as explanations for why our lives are not what we wish. The problem with this line of thinking and living in the past is that it inhibits change and is therefore inherently pessimistic. (p. 163)

5. Understanding our history is important because it shapes who we are. SOMEWHERE BETWEEN IGNORING THE PAST AND WALLOWING IN IT THERE IS A PLACE WHERE WE CAN LEARN FROM WHAT HAS HAPPENED TO US, INCLUDING THE INEVITABLE MISTAKES WE HAVE MADE, AND INTEGRATE THIS KNOWLEDGE INTO OUR PLANS FOR THE FUTURE. (p. 163)

6. THIS PROCESS OF LOOKING, LEARNING, AND LETTING GO INEVITABLY INVOLVES FORGIVENESS AS WE GIVE UP SOME GRIEVANCE TO WHICH WE ARE ENTITLED. (p. 163)

7. Forgiveness is NOT forgetting and it is NOT reconciliation; it is NOT something we do for others; it is something we do for ourselves and requires a high level of emotional and ethical maturity. It is an act of deciding that we want to be liberated

LESSON 71 cont.

from the sense of oppression that accompanies holding a grievance. It is a hopeful statement about our capacity to change. (p. 163-164)

8. When we let go of preoccupations and pseudo-explanations that are rooted in the past, we are free to choose the attitudes with which we confront the present and future....and the key is to remain HOPEFUL. (p. 164)

9. Many people choose a religious basis for their hope; they prefer continual worship to a deity that created us and gave us a set of instructions to follow. (p. 164)

10. Others are skeptical about easy answers to large questions and struggle to establish some basis of meaning for our lives in the face of all its uncertainty. (p. 165)

11. We are all burdened by memories of injury, rejection, or unfairness. Sometimes we refuse to let go of these grievances and become bitter, preoccupied with holding the person or institution responsible. (p. 166)

12. IF EVERY MISFORTUNE CAN BE BLAMED ON SOMEONE ELSE, WE ARE RELIEVED OF THE DIFFICULT TASK OF EXAMINING OUR OWN CONTRIBUTORY BEHAVIOR OR JUST ACCEPTING THE REALITY THAT LIFE IS AND HAS ALWAYS BEEN FULL OF ADVERSITY. WE ALSO MISS OUT ON THE HEALING KNOWLEDGE THAT WHAT HAPPENS TO US IS NOT NEARLY AS IMPORTANT AS THE ATTITUDE WE ADOPT IN RESPONSE. (p. 166)

13. Staying stuck in thoughts of all the slights, insults, rebukes, and unfulfilled dreams, and of all the complaint and scorekeeping in our closest relationships distracts us from the essential question of WHAT DO WE NEED TO DO NOW TO IMPROVE OUR LIVES? (p. 167)

14. What is the point in replaying the past and all its bad drama when we can't change what happened? Why hold onto that outrage and unhappiness??? Much of it is largely a product of our imagination anyway. (p. 167)

LESSON 71 cont.

15. Forgiveness and letting go of the past seem impossibly difficult right up to the moment you actually do it.... (p. 167)

16. DEFINE 'EPITAPH' - a brief poem or other writing in praise of a deceased person. Examples: "He read a lot of magazines." "She started slowly, then backed off." "I told you I was sick." "I'm glad that's over." (p. 168)

REMINDER: Continue work on your SSP.

RECOMMENDED: Practice meditating for 10-15 minutes.

NOTES:

....

....

....

....

....

....

....

....

....

....

....

....

....

....

....

....

LESSON 72

Who PRACTICED MEDITATING and how did it go? What is your biggest challenge with it?

EXPECTATIONS FOR NOTE-TAKING.

REVIEW AND FINISH DISCUSSION on Lesson 71, points 1-16. The point to reiterate here is that we always have a choice about what we focus on and how we remember our past. At any moment, we can ask ourselves 'what do we need to do now to improve our lives?' Letting go and forgiveness seem impossibly difficult right up to the moment we actually do it, and once we do it, we realize how good it feels to truly let go and truly forgive. Unburdened by the past, we can better appreciate and enjoy the present and future.

After DEFINING AND DISCUSSING ideas for epitaphs, have the students begin thinking about their own epitaphs. Remember, unlike a eulogy, epitaphs are short - maybe a line from a poem or a song or something that reflects how you live(d) and how you want to be remembered. An epitaph can be humorous.

HOMEWORK
Go to Lesson 72 Homework in the Journey Workbook, explain directions.
Due tomorrow, 50 points.

REMINDER: Continue work on your SSP.

RECOMMENDED: Practice meditating for 10-15 minutes.

LESSON 72 // HOMEWORK

EPITAPH

Due tomorrow, 50 points.

Write your epitaph (15 words or less) as well as a brief paragraph explaining why you chose this particular epitaph, its significance, and how it reflects the way you want to be remembered.

REMINDER: Continue work on your SSP.

RECOMMENDED: Practice meditating for 10-15 minutes.

NOTES:

....

....

....

....

....

....

....

....

....

....

....

....

....

LESSON 72 // HOMEWORK cont.

EPITAPH HOMEWORK SAMPLE

"STRONG BODY, EASY MIND, OPEN HEART."

This is something I often said at the end of a yoga class and it captures the essence of how I strive to live my life. STRONG BODY is about taking care of myself, eating smart, getting enough sleep, staying active and fit, and making sure I smile and laugh a lot every day. EASY MIND is about not being so reactive but rather calm, relaxed, and confident that everything will be okay, I'll get through it. Easy mind also includes being emotionally clear - not confusing and hard to figure out, there's alignment in my emotions, words, and actions. OPEN HEART is all about love and letting myself out and others in, about sharing, supporting, having compassion, empathy, and gratitude for all aspects of life. All of these - body, mind and heart - humming along and showing up, bring me deep happiness, and an ability to love and experience joy beyond anything I ever imagined.

NOTES:

....

....

....

....

....

....

....

....

....

....

....

LESSON 73

How many of you PRACTICED MEDITATING? How's it going?

SHARE EPITAPHS. Follow this pattern: first, pick a student to read his/her epitaph; second, allow classmates to offer feedback and comment on what they would think and feel if they read the epitaph at their friend's grave; and third, have the student read his/her accompanying paragraph. As usual, it is helpful if you, as teacher, are prepared to go first and set the example. There are no right or wrong answers here, and this is a personal assignment so be mindful of striking the appropriate balance of seriousness, respect, and a sense of humor.

COLLECT EPITAPHS.

DISCUSS THE POSTER PROJECT. Find out how it's going.

HOMEWORK

Finish your SSP. Remember that creativity, neatness, and depth of thinking are all part of your grade. Bring completed poster to class tomorrow and be prepared to share it.

RECOMMENDED: You got it - practice meditating (or some other contemplative activity) for 10-15 minutes.

DROP A HINT... about the final pop quiz.

NOTES:

....

....

....

....

....

....

....

....

....

LESSON 74

Again, check in with those PRACTICING MEDITATION. Encourage them to make it - or some other reflective activity like journal writing - part of their daily routine. The only way to get to know your mind is to sit and watch what it does.

SHARE SSP PROJECTS. Have each student come up to the front, show their poster, introduce it with the title, and read their strategies. After each presentation, allow for positive feedback from the rest of the class. Thoughtful questions are okay - the tone here should be all positive and supportive. Be mindful of the option to simply collect the posters if students just don't want to share them, if it's too personal.

COLLECT POSTERS for grading. See next page, Guidelines for Grading.

HOMEWORK

Practice paying attention to your mind for 10-15 minutes.

NOTES:

....

....

....

....

....

....

....

....

....

....

....

....

....

LESSON 74 cont.

SURVIVAL STRATEGIES POSTER PROJECT

Guidelines for Grading

10 points	followed directions	_____
10 points	neatness	_____
10 points	proper GUM	_____
30 points	creativity	_____
40 points	depth of thinking/content	_____

TOTAL _____

ADDITIONAL COMMENTS:

....

....

....

....

....

....

....

....

....

....

....

....

....

LESSON 75

FINISH SHARING POSTERS, if necessary.
If you finished sharing the posters yesterday, RETURN THE POSTERS AND GRADE SHEETS. Or you can display the posters in the classroom. Eventually it goes in the Pocket Folder along with the grade/comments sheet.

PASS OUT THE POP QUIZ on chapters 25-30, briefly explain the expectations for answering the questions, answer any of your students' questions, and remind them to use complete sentences, proper spelling, and correct grammar.

PAY ATTENTION. If everyone finishes the quiz and there is class time left, go over the quiz together.

COLLECT THE POP QUIZZES for grading and to be returned tomorrow. Along with the other pop quizzes, this one goes in the Pocket Folder when graded/returned.

NOTES:

....

....

....

....

....

....

....

....

....

....

....

....

....

....

LESSON 75 // POP QUIZ

POP QUIZ #5 ON CHAPTERS 25-30

50 points

Answer the following questions to the best of your ability. Proper grammar and spelling count. Write on the back, if needed.

1. List some of the things that define us?

2. What role does fear play in our personal lives and why is this good or bad?

3. Explain the "narcissistic myth" of parenting.

4. What creates cynicism?

5. What is the primary task of parenting?

6. What is set up when we become nostalgic?

7. Define 'memory.'

8. Why is laughter so important?

9. _ e _ _ _ _   _ _ _ _ t _   is a function of   _ _ o _ _ _.

10. Explain the difference between 'forgiveness' and 'letting go.'

LESSON 75 // POP QUIZ cont.

POP QUIZ #5 SAMPLE ANSWER KEY

1. Some of the things that define us are what we pay attention to, what we worry about, and how we interpret what happens to us.

2. We are often driven by a fear of failure and think material wealth is a measure of our success. We're so focused on accumulating money that we're distracted from the people and activities that give more lasting pleasure and satisfaction.

3. The "narcissistic myth" of parenting is the idea that parents think they are solely responsible for their children's successes and failures. Children succeed or fail primarily because of their own good or bad decisions about how they will live their lives.

4. We create cynicism when there are major contradictions between what we say and what we do. Ultimately, children are responsible for how they incorporate what they saw and learned in childhood.

5. The primary task of parenting, beyond attending to the day-to-day physical and emotional welfare of our kids, is to convey a sense that our kids can be happy in an uncertain and imperfect world. Parents do this by example. Be an optimist.

6. If we are too nostalgic, we think everything was better in the past and so we're not as present or as happy with what's going on now. Clinging to an idealized vision of the past insures dissatisfaction with the present. We have a choice to accept and enjoy what we made of our lives or to be cynical.

7. Memory is a story we tell ourselves about the past that is full of distortions, wishful thinking, and unfulfilled dreams. What we remember and how we remember it are affected by the meaning and effort we use to understand ourselves.

8. Laughter is a significant component and indicator of a happy life.

9. M - e - n - t - a - l h - e - a - l - t - h is a function of c - h - o - i - c - e.

LESSON 75 // POP QUIZ cont.

10. Letting go of outdated preoccupations and pseudo-explanations frees us to choose our attitude about the future. Be hopeful. Letting go involves forgiveness when we are giving up some grievance that we are entitled to. We don't necessarily forget or reconcile, and we don't do it for others. Forgiveness is something we do for ourselves because we don't want to carry the oppressive feeling anymore.

NOTES:

....

....

....

....

....

....

....

....

....

....

....

....

....

....

....

....

....

OVERVIEW

LESSONS 76-80

HOMEWORK ASSIGNMENTS (1)
- Journey Workbook/Pocket Folder Check #3

FINAL EXAM

COURSE CONCLUSION

COURSE EVALUATION

ABOUT THE AUTHOR

LESSON 76

RETURN GRADED POP QUIZZES. Discuss any questions. Keep in Pocket Folder.

Use this entire class to COMPLETE JOURNEY WORKBOOK/POCKET FOLDER CHECK #3. Students may work in pairs as they organize all their notes and assignments and make a list of anything that is missing. Walk around the room, making sure to spend time with every student and get a feel for the completeness of their written coursework. Use the last 10-15 minutes of class to assess points out of 50 and record in grade book. If anything is missing, follow up with those students tomorrow or the next day.

RECOMMENDED: Meditate or write in a journal for 10-15 minutes.

HOMEWORK
Begin reviewing your course materials for the Final Exam.

NOTES:

....

....

....

....

....

....

....

....

....

....

....

....

....

LESSON 76 // JOURNEY CHECKLIST #3

- **JW/PF CHECK #1**

- **JW/PF CHECK #2**

- **LESSON 51** Notes and Reflections on Chapter 22

- **LESSONS 52 & 53** Notes and Reflections on Chapter 23

- **LESSON 53** Homework - Letter about Criticism or Gratitude

- **LESSONS 55 & 56** Notes and Reflections on Chapter 24

- **POP QUIZ #4** (Pocket Folder)

- **LESSONS 58 & 59** Notes and Reflections on Chapter 25

- **LESSON 59** Homework - 100 Words on Meditation

- **LESSONS 60 & 61** Notes and Reflections on Chapter 26

- **LESSON 61** Homework - Role Models

- **LESSONS 62 & 63** Notes and Reflections on Chapter 27

- **LESSON 63** Homework - Eulogy

- **LESSONS 65 & 66** Notes and Reflections on Chapter 28

- **LESSON 66** Homework - Jokes

- **LESSONS 68 & 69** Notes and Reflections on Chapter 29

- **LESSONS 71 & 72** Notes and Reflections on Chapter 30

- **LESSON 72** Homework - Epitaph

- **COMPLETED SURVIVAL STRATEGIES POSTER** and grade sheet (Pocket Folder)

- **POP QUIZ #5** (Pocket Folder)

- **FINAL EXAM** (Pocket Folder)

INITIAL/DATE COMPLETE _____/_____

POINTS OUT OF 50_____

LESSON 77

FOLLOW UP ON THE JW/PF CHECK for those students who had an incomplete yesterday. Record grades.

IN PREPARATION FOR THE FINAL EXAM, spend the entire class reviewing the course. Go chapter by chapter, read each title, review the main points from note-taking, answer any questions, make practical connections to their everyday lives, review the pop quizzes.....get them talking to stimulate their thinking about what they've learned in the course and how they are applying this knowledge in their daily lives. AIM TO COMPLETE THIS OVER-VIEW IN TWO CLASS PERIODS. This exercise could be done in small groups.

Because the Final Exam isn't about regurgitating memorized facts, names, and dates, really the best way for your students to prepare for it is to be familiar with the concepts covered in the course and how they relate to them individually. The exam is an opportunity to dem-onstrate their understanding of personality and behavior, their understanding of themselves and how they show up in various relationships, what they want to cultivate and what they want to avoid, how they will incorporate their increased awareness across their lives going forward..... Really, it's all about the quality of their thinking and their ability to pay attention to all of the components of learning happiness.

HOMEWORK
Review your JW/PF and spend 15 minutes meditating or journal writing.

NOTES:

....

....

....

....

....

....

....

....

LESSON 78

Use this class period to continue and complete the COURSE REVIEW. See notes from yesterday's lesson for guidelines.

The FINAL EXAM IS TOMORROW. It is an essay exam so come prepared to talk to me, the teacher, on paper for the entire class period.

HOMEWORK

Do whatever you need to do to prepare for tomorrow's Final Exam. Being familiar with the contents of your JW/PF will be helpful....and then just relax, get a good night's sleep, and show up 100% tomorrow.

NOTE ABOUT THE FINAL

Prepare your Final Exams by stapling at least 5 sheets of college-ruled notebook paper to the exam. Have extra sharpened pencils on hand.

NOTES:

....

....

....

....

....

....

....

....

....

....

....

....

LESSON 79

TAKE THE FINAL EXAM. Pencils sharp, course materials away. Explain that the exam is an essay question and they will spend the entire class writing. Neatness, proper grammar, spelling and mechanics, organization, and clarity of thinking all count towards their grade. Suggest writing an outline to organize thoughts and ideas.

PASS OUT THE PREPARED FINAL EXAM (stapled to at least 5 pieces of lined notebook paper). Go over the essay question, and begin. Spend the class floating, paying attention. Be available if they have questions.

REMIND THEM when there are 10 minutes left. Then again at 5 minutes remaining.

COLLECT FINAL EXAMS for grading and to be returned for discussion tomorrow. This is a quick turn-around; don't let it compromise the quality of your comments/evaluation. If it's too quick and depending on your timing/situation, you can make a different arrangement.

NOTES:

....

....

....

....

....

....

....

....

....

....

....

....

....

....

LESSON 79 // FINAL EXAM

FINAL EXAM

100 Points

Answer the following essay question: HOW WILL YOU PURSUE HAPPINESS?

Frame your answer in terms of what you want to make of your relationships, what you want to make of your education, and what you want to make of your career. How do you *see* it all playing out? You can talk about your dreams and goals, what you want to avoid, what you want to focus on and bring into your life, things you'll try to remember about the course, how the course changed you, how you'll handle the inevitable difficult, unexpected or tragic experiences life will serve up. Basically, your answer articulates your roadmap, your philosophy and attitude, the tools in your toolbox, how you envision finding your way and creating a happy life.

GUIDELINES FOR GRADING

10 points	neatness, spelling, proper GUM
15 points	organization (make an outline if it helps)
75 points	clarity and depth of thinking

NOTES:

....

....

....

....

....

....

....

....

....

....

LESSON 79 // FINAL EXAM cont.

SAMPLE

OUTLINE

<u>Relationships</u>

- with family
- with friends
- marriage/divorce
- being a parent

<u>Education</u>

- college and graduate school
- lifelong learning
- health and fitness

<u>Career</u>

- classroom teacher
- volunteer/community - school, non-profit organizations
- hobbies
- writing

<u>Dreams/Focus</u>

- role of optimism, courage, hope
- laughter and enjoyment
- ease and patience
- stay awake!!

One of the most important ideas I learned in this class is that the quality of my relationships is a significant determinant in the quality of my life and how happy I am. And, if I hope to attract people worthy of cherishing, I must cultivate desirable attributes in myself. I am very grateful and fortunate to have parents who taught me, especially by example, so many of these desirable attributes. They taught me about honesty, doing my best, and working hard at anything I do. They taught me the importance of getting a good education and being curious about the world. My mom especially taught me about caring, affection, listening, and patience. They were both active and fit and made healthy choices so I learned and continue to enjoy a very healthy lifestyle. In short, I benefitted tremendously from my mom and dad, and I know I'm a better person/parent for what I learned from them. They gave me a great start to go out and experience life and find my way.

LESSON 79 // FINAL EXAM cont.

I grew up in the middle of two brothers. My older brother died, much too young from brain cancer, and I have struggled to come to terms with losing him, the unfairness of such a random fate. Nothing is the same. With time my sadness will soften. Thanks to having two brothers, there's tomboy in me, I'm a hard worker, and I don't mind getting dirty, which helped create an overlap in our interests. But I also learned to remind them of the female perspective. Being on good terms with my family is important to me, and I will sit down and stay put through whatever tough conversations we need to have to understand each other better and remain close. I know important things take time and patience. I've learned to accept that some things can't be changed.

It's important to me to be a good friend - reliable, trustworthy, fun, a good listener, nonjudgmental. While I'm not really the kind of person to have lots of friends, I enjoy being friendly and having a handful of really close friends. I'm a pretty private person, don't go much for gossip and superficiality, I tend to like women who talk about "real" things, what's really going on. I just like connecting. Girlfriends provide a healthy dimension, serious and fun - so many shared experiences that often men just don't get....and that's okay. I cherish girl time.

Because I didn't observe the happiest marriage between my mom and dad, I was pretty clueless when it came to dating and picking a person. I filled in a lot of blanks myself, often incorrectly, assuming that familiarity in one area - like education - meant familiarity/similarity in other areas. I found out the hard way because I didn't start figuring things out until after I married the guy and had two kids. I kept making the best of it, but I didn't recognize myself in the picture. It was an unhappy chapter that ultimately led to a lot of really important learning.

While I never envisioned a divorce in my life plan, it became clear that it was necessary. With the help of an excellent therapist, I went back into my childhood to understand what happened to me, how my parents' parenting affected me both positively and negatively. She helped me make sense of what I needed to let go of and what behaviors I could learn to manage better, what I could pull up and strengthen. I've never worked so hard in my life - it was brutal at times - and absolutely the best thing that ever happened to me. My life makes so much sense to me now. I still ended up divorced because too many things were wrong

LESSON 79 // FINAL EXAM cont.

about that relationship. But I've moved on, I started over, I'm a better (i.e. more authentic) mom to my sons, I'm happier from a much more knowing place. I think I'm doing a good job being a steady, healthy role model for my sons. In addition to their daily care-giving needs, I teach by example - how to listen nonjudgmentally, to not be so reactive or take things too personally, I show them they are safe to express their feelings, I show them that if we stay put when we'd rather run away, we can resolve just about anything. I also show them that when bad things happen, we have a choice in how we interpret it and assign meaning, and that our choice largely determines how happy we are going forward. It all works - we have wonderful relationships, they're very skilled and tuned into who they are and to not getting bogged down in negativity. Above all, we have fun together and we laugh a lot.

Education will always be important to me whether I'm in a classroom or not. I learn a lot by reading and having a variety of hobbies and interests, by being curious, by enjoying other people and hearing their stories. The way I see it, there's always more to learn, to see, to do, and I enjoy keeping my world big and open, to trying new things. It keeps things interesting and fun. Staying fit and active is hugely important, and I'm not afraid of hard work. But it's a balance - life isn't all work and self-improvement, it's also about enjoyment and relaxing.

I enjoyed my years as a classroom teacher. I love kids and I love figuring out how to connect with and motivate them. In the classroom, I really learned that enthusiasm is contagious..... and the importance of patience. Everyone learns at a different pace and that's okay. Being a teacher was a great environment to practice being a positive role model of desirable attributes. When conflicts arose, I'd sit with them until the issue was resolved to everyone's satisfaction; everyone was heard; they learned about compromise, flexibility, and empathy; they learned not to take everything so personally.

And this experience translated beautifully to parenting. I LOVE being a mom and look forward to being a grandma one day! It's important to me to have something worthwhile to do with my time, something that really motivates me, and I've found various projects over the years that sustain me in that way while being a full-time mom. Writing the Pursuit of Happiness curriculum has been an excellent and challenging project - it pulls together so many things that are meaningful to me, and I get excited imagining kids becoming more aware and more skilled in their relationships and about whom to pick. I love the idea of

LESSON 79 // FINAL EXAM cont.

giving young people a better shot at being happy. If I decide to self-publish and/or put the course online, then I'll have more new things to learn and that's all good.

So when I look back at the first several decades of my life, I understand why it went the way it went. My parents gave me a good start, I had some painful trial and error learning. I'm not mad about that and I don't blame anyone for it. They did the best they could and I accept responsibility for how I carried my childhood patterns into my adult life. It had to play out so I could learn from it....and I have indeed learned a ton. I look ahead to the next several decades and I'm full of hope. Taking an honest look requires courage, patience, and determination. A handful of important people did an excellent job of selling hope and helping me to keep believing my life would eventually all come together.

Having said all that, I guess I just really love my life, all of it.....because it got me to this place. And life keeps happening and I'll do my best to keep responding as optimistically and compassionately as I can. I don't want to sound like a pollyanna and like everything is perfect all the time - it's not. I hit rough patches, we get sideways in our relationships. But I do trust that I can and will work through things, and that we'll come out of it alright, even stronger. Above all, I want to stay mindful of living every moment, to being present, right here, right now. After all these years, I can honestly say I'll recognize the warning signs if I start to fall asleep at the wheel. Growing older has some definite perks too - the sense of accomplishment, the relaxing, the appreciation for how fortunate I've been to live this life... things that are way more important than gray hairs and wrinkles.

I've learned happiness.

LESSON 80

RETURN GRADED FINAL EXAMS. Spend part of this class discussing the Final Exam and (optional) invite students to share parts of their essay. Be compassionate and supportive, enthusiastic and optimistic.....this is personal stuff and each student should be celebrated for their individuality and their goals.

GO TO the REFLECTION PAGES in their Journey Workbook. These pages provide an opportunity to check in, take a closer look, determine course corrections, etc. one, five, ten, twenty-five, and fifty years out. Keep paying attention to your happiness!!

COURSE EVALUATION - A sample course evaluation is included. Feel free to modify it to suit your needs. Students can snail-mail a hard copy or reply via email, or you could ask for their feedback orally. You decide.

If this is your final class, end on an upbeat and encouraging note. Share some highlights and low-lights, some particularly funny or memorable experiences, pull it all together for them. Find your words to express what teaching the course meant to you.

We're all on a journey and parts of the journey are universally shared experiences - graduations, marriages, divorces, births, deaths, raising children, careers starting/changing/ ending, illness, tragedy. Along the way, we struggle. Along the way, we can keep getting smarter and pay more attention and learn from the pain of our mistakes. Along the way, we really can be happy - not every second of every minute of every day. BUT WE CAN GIVE THE PURSUIT OF HAPPINESS OUR BEST EFFORT EACH DAY. IT IS INDEED A WORTHY PURSUIT.

If you still have time, this is an opportunity to watch a movie together. "The Bucket List" tops my list for an inspirational, fun and funny, honest, pulling-it-all-together message with which to send your students on their way.

LESSON 80 // COURSE EVALUATION

Overall, what do you think of The Pursuit of Happiness course and would you recommend it to others? Please explain.

....

....

....

....

What did you find particularly helpful/practical?

....

....

....

....

How would you change the course - format, content, assignments, etc? Please be specific.

....

....

....

....

Additional comments:

....

....

....

....

I appreciate your feedback as I continue improving the course for future students.
MAKE IT A BOLD AND FULFILLING JOURNEY!!

ABOUT THE AUTHOR

Robin Patterson has been consciously pursuing happiness for about a decade. A Stanford-educated teacher, she is a full-time mom, and rounds out her days being a school and community volunteer, a gardener, a keeper of chickens, a yogi-runner-skier-river floater, an avid reader, and, hopefully, an inspiration to others to live each day to the fullest. Robin lives on a farm in Bozeman, Montana with her two teenage sons and a variety of entertaining animals. The skies are big, the mountains are reassuring, the people are friendly, and life is good.

Robin is grateful for the many special people who have supported and helped her along the way. She welcomes your feedback on *The Pursuit of Happiness* curriculum in particular, and pursuing happiness in general.

Please visit her website at: www.LRNhappiness.com

ONE YEAR LATER...

HOW'S YOUR PURSUIT OF HAPPINESS JOURNEY GOING?

....

....

....

....

....

....

....

....

....

....

....

....

....

....

....

....

....

....

....

....

ONE YEAR LATER...

FIVE YEARS LATER...

HOW'S YOUR PURSUIT OF HAPPINESS JOURNEY GOING? WHAT DOES YOUR LIFE LOOK LIKE NOW? RE-READ YOUR FINAL EXAM AND COMPARE.

....

....

....

....

....

....

....

....

....

....

....

....

....

....

....

....

....

....

....

FIVE YEARS LATER...

TEN YEARS LATER...

HOW'S YOUR PURSUIT OF HAPPINESS JOURNEY GOING? WHAT DOES YOUR LIFE LOOK LIKE NOW? RE-READ YOUR FINAL EXAM AND COMPARE. IF YOU'RE ON TRACK, WHY? IF YOU'RE NOT ON TRACK, WHY NOT? WHAT CHANGES DO YOU NEED TO MAKE RIGHT NOW?

TEN YEARS LATER...

TWENTY-FIVE YEARS LATER...

SO HOW'S IT ALL GOING?

_____

_____

_____

_____

_____

_____

_____

_____

_____

_____

_____

_____

_____

_____

_____

_____

_____

_____

_____

_____

_____

_____

TWENTY-FIVE YEARS LATER...

FIFTY YEARS LATER...

SO, HOW WOULD YOU WRITE YOUR EULOGY TODAY, ALL THESE YEARS LATER? HOW ARE YOU DOING WITH AGING? IN SPITE OF LIFE'S UNCERTAINTY, HAVE YOU FOUND HAPPINESS? TELL YOUR STORY.

FIFTY YEARS LATER...

BE HAPPY.

Made in the USA
Middletown, DE
16 September 2021